IELTS Course Material

(Reading)

Developed By

Atik Rahman

BA(hons)English,MA(English), India

Founder & Chairman, MasterMind.

Former IELTS Trainer at ATM's

Former IELTS Trainer at S@ifur's Pvt Ltd.

Former IELTS Trainer at Uttara Ideal College, Dhaka, Bangladesh.

READING PASSAGE 01

POPULATION VIABILITY ANALYSIS

You should spend about 20 minutes on Questions 1-12 which are based on Reading Passage 1 below:

Part A

To make political decisions about the extent and type of forestry in a region it is important to understand the consequences of those decisions. One tool for assessing the impact of forestry on the ecosystem is population viability analysis (PVA). This is a tool for predicting the probability that a species will become extinct in a particular region over a specific period. It has been successfully used in the United States to provide input into resource exploitation decisions and assist wildlife managers and there is now an enormous potential for using population viability to assist wildlife management in Australia's forests. A species becomes extinct when the last individual dies. This observation is a useful starting point for any discussion of extinction as it highlights the role of luck and chance in the extinction process. To make a prediction about extinction we need to understand the processes that can contribute to it and these fall into four broad categories which are discussed below.

Part B

A) Early attempts to predict population viability were based on demographic uncertainty whether an individual survives from one year to the next will largely be a matter of chance. Some pairs may produce several young in a single year while others may produce none in that same year. Small populations will fluctuate enormously because of the random nature of birth and death and these chance fluctuations can cause species extinctions even if, on average, the population size should increase. Taking only this uncertainty of ability to reproduce into account, extinction is unlikely if the number of individuals in a population is above about 50 and the population is growing.

B) Small populations cannot avoid a certain amount of inbreeding. This is particularly true if there is a very small number of one sex. For example, if there are only 20 individuals of a species and only one is a male, all future individuals in the species must be descended from that one male. For most animal species such individuals are less likely to survive and reproduce. Inbreeding increases the chance of extinction.

C) Variation within a species is the raw material upon which natural selection acts. Without genetic variability, a species lacks the capacity to evolve and cannot adapt to changes in its environment or to new predators and new diseases. The loss of genetic diversity associated with reductions in population size will contribute to the likelihood of extinction.

D) Recent research has shown that other factors need to be considered. Australia's environment fluctuates enormously from year to year. These fluctuations add yet another degree of uncertainty to the survival of many species. Catastrophes such as fire, flood, drought or epidemic may reduce population sizes to a small fraction of their average level. When allowance is made for these two additional elements of uncertainty the population size necessary to be confident of persistence for a few hundred years may increase to several thousand.

Part C

Besides these processes, we need to bear in mind the distribution of a population. A species that occurs in five isolated places each containing 20 individuals will not have the same probability of extinction as a species with a single population of 100 individuals in a single locality. Where logging occurs (that is, the cutting down of forests for timber) forest-dependent creatures in that area will be forced to leave. Ground-dwelling herbivores may return within a decade. However, arboreal marsupials (that is animals which live in trees) may not recover to pre-logging densities for over a century. As more forests are logged, animal population sizes will be reduced further. Regardless of the theory or model that we choose, a reduction in population size decreases the genetic diversity of a population and increases the probability of extinction because of any or all of the processes listed above. It is, therefore, a scientific fact that increasing the area that is loaded in any region will increase the probability that forest-dependent animals will become extinct.

Questions 1-4:

Do the following statements agree with the views of the writer in *Part A* of Reading Passage 1?

In boxes 1-4 on your answer sheet write:

YES   if the statement agrees with the writer
NO   if the statement contradicts the writer
NOT GIVEN   if it is impossible to say what the writer thinks about this

Example: A link exists between the consequences of decisions and the decision-making process itself. Answer: YES.

1. Scientists are interested in the effect of forestry on native animals.
2. PVA has been used in Australia for many years.

3. A species is said to be extinct when only one individual exists.
4. Extinction is a naturally occurring phenomenon.

Questions 5-8:

These questions are based on *Part B* of Reading Passage 1.

In paragraphs A to D the author describes four processes which may
contribute to the extinction of a species.
Match the list of processes (i-vi) to the paragraphs.
Write the appropriate number (i-vi) in boxes 5-8 on your answer sheet.
*NB. There are more processes than paragraphs so you will not use all of
them.*

Paragraphs   Processes
5. Paragraph A   i Loss of ability to adapt
6. Paragraph B   ii Natural disasters
7. Paragraph C   iii An imbalance of the sexes
8. Paragraph D   iv Human disasters
                                 v Evolution
                                 vi The haphazard nature of reproduction

Questions 9-11:
Based on your reading of Part C, complete the sentences below.
Use NO MORE THAN THREE WORDS for each answer.
Write your answers in boxes 9-11 on your answer sheet.
While the population of a species may be on the increase, there is always a
chance that small isolated groups.......... (9).......... Survival of a species
depends on a balance between the size of a population and it's..........
(10)......... The likelihood that animals which live in forests will become
extinct is increased when.......... (11)...........
Question 12:
Choose the appropriate letter A-D and write it in box 12 on your answer
sheet.
12. An alternative heading for the passage could be:

    A. The protection of native flora and fauna
    B. Influential factors in assessing survival probability
    C. An economic rationale for the logging of forests
    D. Preventive measures for the extinction of a species

Visual Symbols and the Blind

You should spend no more than 20 minutes on Questions 27-40 which are based on Reading Passage 2 below.

From a number of recent studies, it has become clear that blind people can appreciate the use of outlines and perspectives to describe the

Fig. 1

arrangement of objects and other surfaces in space.

But pictures are more than literal representations. This fact was drawn to my attention dramatically when a blind woman in one of my investigations decided on her own initiative to draw a wheel as it was spinning. To show this motion, she traced a curve inside the circle (Fig. 1). I was taken aback, lines of motion, such as the one she used, are a very recent invention in the history of illustration. Indeed, as art scholar David Kunzle notes, Wilhelm Busch, a trend-setting nineteenth-century cartoonist, used virtually no motion lines in his popular figure until about 1877.

When I asked several other blind study subjects to draw a spinning wheel, one particularly clever rendition appeared repeatedly: several subjects showed the wheel's spokes as curves lines. When asked about these curves, they all described them as metaphorical ways of suggesting motion. Majority rule would argue that this device somehow indicated motion very well. But was it a better indicator than, say, broken or wavy lines or any other kind of line, for that matter? The answer was not clear. So I decided to test whether various lines of motion were apt ways of showing movement or if they were merely idiosyncratic marks. Moreover, I wanted to discover whether there were differences in how the blind and the sighted interpreted lines of motion.

To search out these answers, I created raised-line drawings of five different wheels, depicting spokes with lines that curved, bent, waved, dashed and extended beyond the perimeters of the wheel. I then asked eighteen blind volunteers to feel the wheels and assign one of the following motions to each wheel: wobbling, spinning fast, spinning steadily, jerking or braking. My control group consisted of eighteen sighted undergraduates from the University of Toronto.

All but one of the blind subjects assigned distinctive motions to each wheel. Most guessed that the curved spokes indicated that the wheel was spinning steadily; the wavy spokes, they thought; suggested that the wheel was wobbling, and the bent spokes were taken as a sign that the wheel was jerking. Subjects assumed that spokes extending beyond the wheel's perimeter signified that the wheel had its brakes on and that dashed spokes indicated the wheel was spinning quickly.

In addition, the favored description for the sighted was favored description for the blind in every instance. What is more, the consensus among the sighted was barely higher than that among the blind. Because motion devices are unfamiliar to the blind, the task I gave them involved some problem solving. Evidently, however, the blind not only figured out the meaning for each of the motion, but as a group they generally came up with the same meaning at least as frequently as did sighted subjects.

Part 2
We have found that the blind understand other kinds of visual metaphors as well. One blind woman drew a picture of a child inside a heart-choosing that symbol, she said, to show that love surrounded the child. With Chang Hong Liu, a doctoral student from china, I have begun exploring how well blind people understand the symbolism behind shapes such as hearts that do not directly represent their meaning.

We gave a list of twenty pairs of words to sighted subjects and asked them to pick from each pair the term that best related to a circle and the term that best related to assure. For example, we asked: what goes with soft? A circle or a square? Which shape goes with hard?

Words associated among with circle/square	Agreement among subjects(%)
SOFT-HARD	100
MOTHER-FATHER	94
HAPPY-SAD	94
GOOD-EVIL	89
LOVE-HATE	89
ALIVE-DEAD	87
BRIGHT-DARK	87
LIGHT-HEAVY	85
WARM-COLD	81
SUMMER-WINTER	81
WEAK-STRONG	79
FAST-SLOW	79
CAT-DOG	74
SPRING-FALL	74
QUIET-LOUD	62
WALKING-STANDING	62
ODD-EVEN	57
FAR-NEAR	53
PLANT-ANIMAL	53
DEEP-SHALLOW	51

Fig. 2- Subjects were asked which word in each pair fits with a circle and which with a square. These percentages show the level of consensus among sighted subjects.

All our subjects deemed the circle soft and the square hard. A full 94% ascribed happy to the circle, instead of sad. But other pairs revealed less agreement: 79% matched fast to slow and weak to strong, respectively.

And only 51% linked deep to circle and shallow to square. (*See Fig. 2*)
When we tested four totally blind volunteers using the same list, we found
that their choices closely resembled those made by the sighted subjects.
One man, who had been blind since birth, scored extremely well. He made
only one match differing from the consensus, assigning 'far' to square and
'near' to circle. In fact, only a small majority of sighted subjects, 53%, had
paired far and near to the opposite partners. Thus we concluded that the
blind interprets abstract shapes as sighted people do.
Questions:
Choose the correct letter, A, B, C or D.
Write your answers in boxes 27 –29 on your answer sheet.

27 In the first paragraph, the writer makes the point that blind people
        A. May be interested in studying art.
        B. can draw outlines of different objects and surfaces.
        C. can recognize conventions such as perspective.
        D. can draw accurately.
28 The writer was surprised because the blind woman
        A. Drew a circle on her own initiative.
        B. did not understand what a wheel looked like.
        C. included a symbol representing movement.
        D. was the first person to use lines of motion.

29 From the experiment described in Part 1, the writer found that the blind
subjects
        A. Had good understanding of symbols representing movement.
        B. could control the movement of wheels very accurately.
        C. worked together well as a group in solving problems.
        D. got better results than the sighted undergraduates.

Questions 30 –32
Look at the following diagrams (Questions 30 –32), and the list of types of
movement below. Match each diagram to the type of movement A–
E generally assigned to it in the experiment. Choose the correct letter A–
E and write them in boxes 30–32 on your answer sheet.

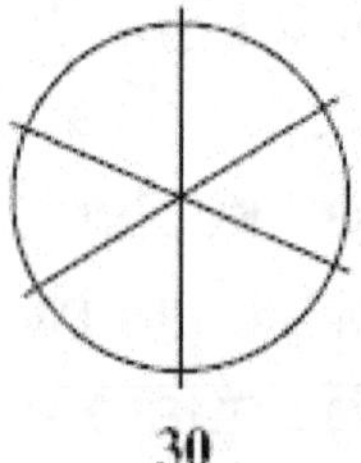
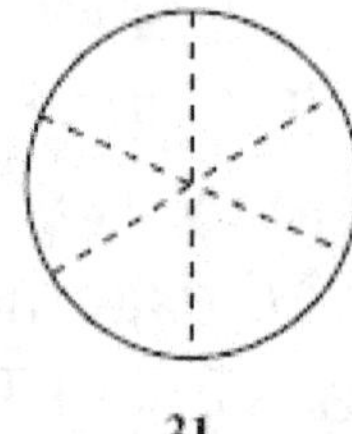
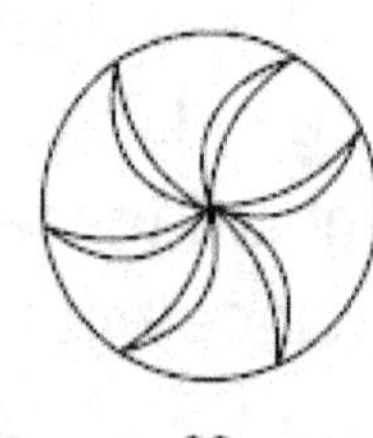

30   31   32

A   steady spinning

B   jerky movement

C   rapid spinning

D   wobbling movement

E   use of brakes

Questions 33 –39
complete the summary below using words from the box. Write your answers in boxes 33 –39 on your answer sheet. NB You may use any word more than once.

In the experiment described in Part 2, a set of word 33.............. was used to investigate whether blind and sighted people perceived the symbolism in abstract 34.............. in the same way. Subjects were asked which word fitted best with a circle and which with a square. From the 35.........… volunteers, everyone thought a circle fitted 'soft 'while a square fitted 'hard'. However, only 51% of the 36.............. volunteers assigned a circle to 37............ When the test was later repeated with 38............ volunteers, it was found that they made 39............ choices.

associations	blind	deep	hard
hundred	identical	pairs	
shapes	sighted	similar	shallow
soft	words		

Question 40
Choose the correct letter A, B, C or D. Write your answer in box 40 on your answer sheet.
Which of the following statements best summarizes the writer's general conclusion?
 A The blind represent some aspects of reality differently from sighted people.
 B The blind comprehend visual metaphors in similar ways to sighted people.
 C The blind may create unusual and effective symbols to represent reality.
 D The blind may be successful artists if given the right training.

READING PASSAGE 03

Zoo Conservation Programmers

You should spend about 20 minutes on Questions 16-28 which are based on Reading Passage 3 below.

One of London Zoo's recent advertisements caused me some irritation, so patently did it distort reality. Headlined "Without zoos, you might as well tell these animals to get stuffed", it was bordered with illustrations of several endangered species and went on to extol the myth that without zoos like London Zoo these animals "will almost certainly disappear forever". With the zoo world's rather mediocre record on conservation, one might be forgiven for being slightly skeptical about such an advertisement.

Zoos were originally created as places of entertainment, and their suggested involvement with conservation didn't seriously arise until about 30 years ago, when the Zoological Society of London held the first formal international meeting on the subject. Eight years later, a series of world conferences took place, entitled "The Breeding of Endangered Species", and from this point onwards conservation became the zoo community's buzzword. This commitment has now been clear defined in The World Zoo

Conservation Strategy (WZCS, September 1993), which although an important and welcome document does seem to be based on an unrealistic optimism about the nature of the zoo industry.

The WZCS estimates that there are about 10,000 zoos in the world, of which around 1,000 represent a core of quality collections capable of participating in coordinated conservation programmers. This is probably the document's first failing, as I believe that 10,000 is a serious underestimate of the total number of places masquerading as zoological establishments. Of course, it is difficult to get accurate data but, to put the issue into perspective, I have found that, in a year of working in Eastern Europe, I discover fresh zoos on almost a weekly basis.

The second flaw in the reasoning of the WZCS document is the naive faith it places in its 1,000 core zoos. One would assume that the caliber of these institutions would have been carefully examined, but it appears that the criterion for inclusion on this select list might merely be that the zoo is a member of a zoo federation or association. This might be a good starting point, working on the premise that members must meet certain standards, but again the facts don't support the theory. The greatly respected American Association of Zoological Parks and Aquariums (AAZPA) has had extremely dubious members, and in the UK the Federation of Zoological Gardens of Great Britain and Ireland has

Occasionally had members that have been roundly censured in the national press. These include Robin Hill Adventure Park on the Isle of Wight, which many considered the most notorious collection of animals in the country. This establishment, which for years was protected by the Isle's local council (which viewed it as a tourist amenity), was finally closed down following a damning report by a veterinary inspector appointed under the terms of the Zoo Licensing Act 1981. As it was always a collection of dubious repute, one is obliged to reflect upon the standards that the Zoo Federation sets when granting membership. The situation is even worse in developing countries where little money is available for redevelopment and it is hard to see a way of incorporating collections into the overall scheme of the

WZCS.

Even assuming that the WZCS's 1,000 core zoos are all of a high standard complete with scientific staff and research facilities, trained and dedicated keepers, accommodation that permits normal or natural behavior, and a policy of co-operating fully with one another what might be the potential for conservation? Colin Trudge, author of Last Animals at the Zoo (Oxford University Press, 1992), argues that "if the world's zoos worked together in co-operative breeding programmers, then even without further expansion they could save around 2,000 species of endangered land vertebrates'. This seems an extremely optimistic proposition from a man who must be aware of the failings and weaknesses of the zoo industry the man who, when a member of the council of London Zoo, had to persuade the zoo to devote more of its activities to conservation. Moreover, where are the facts to support such optimism?

Today approximately 16 species might be said to have been "saved" by captive breeding programmers, although a number of these can hardly be looked upon as resounding successes. Beyond that, about a further 20 species are being seriously considered for zoo conservation programmers. Given that the international conference at London Zoo was held 30 years ago, this is pretty slow progress, and a long way off Trudge's target of 2,000.

Do the following statements agree with the views of the writer in Reading Passage 3? In boxes 16-22 write:
    Y   if the statement agrees with the writer
    N   if the statement contradicts the writer
    NG if it is impossible to say what the writer thinks about this

16.   London Zoo's advertisements are dishonest.
17.   Zoos made an insignificant contribution to conservation up until 30 years ago.
18.   The WZCS document is not known in Eastern Europe.

19.   Zoos in the WZCS select list were carefully inspected.
20.   No-one knew how the animals were being treated at Robin Hill
Adventure Park.
21.   Colin Tudge was dissatisfied with the treatment of animals at London
Zoo.
22.   The number of successful zoo conservation programmers is
unsatisfactory.

Questions 23-25
Choose the appropriate letters A-D and write them in boxes 23-25 on your
answer sheet.

23 What were the objectives of the WZCS document?
   A.   to improve the calibre of zoos worldwide
   B.   to identify zoos suitable for conservation practice
   C.   to provide funds for zoos in underdeveloped countries
   D.   to list the endangered species of the world

24 Why does the writer refer to Robin Hill Adventure Park?
   A.   to support the Isle of Wight local council
   B.   to criticize the 1981 Zoo Licensing Act
   C.   to illustrate a weakness in the WZCS document
   D.   to exemplify the standards in AAZPA zoos

25 What word best describes the writer's response to Colin Tudges'
prediction on captive breeding programmers?
   A.   disbelieving
   B.   Impartial
   C.   Prejudiced
   D.   Accepting

Questions 26-28
the writer mentions a number of factors which lead him to doubt the value
of the WZCS document Which THREE of the following factors are
mentioned? Write your answers (A-F) in boxes 26-28 on your answer

sheet.

List of Factors:
A. the number of unregistered zoos in the world
B. the lack of money in developing countries
C. the actions of the Isle of Wight local council
D. the failure of the WZCS to examine the standards of the "core zoos"
E. the unrealistic aim of the WZCS in view of the number of species "saved" to date
F. the policies of WZCS zoo managers

READING PASSAGE 04

A Workaholic Economy

You should spend about 20 minutes on Questions 27-38 which are based on Reading Passage 4 below.

For the first century or so of the industrial revolution, increased productivity led to decreases in working hours. Employees who had been putting in 12-hour days, six days a week, found their time on the job shrinking to 10 hours daily, then finally to eight hours, five days a week. Only a generation ago social planners worried about what people would do with all this new-found free time. In the US, at least it seems they need not have bothered.

Although the output per hour of work has more than doubled since 1945, leisure seems reserved largely for the unemployed and underemployed. Those who work full-time spend as much time on the job as they did at the end of World War II. In fact, working hours have increased noticeably since 1970 — perhaps because real wages have stagnated since that year. Bookstores now abound with manuals describing how to manage time and cope with stress.

There are several reasons for lost leisure. Since 1979, companies have responded to improvements in the business climate by having employees work overtime rather than by hiring extra personnel, says economist Juliet B. Schor of Harvard University. Indeed, the current economic recovery has gained a certain amount of notoriety for its "jobless" nature: increased production has been almost entirely decoupled from employment. Some firms are even downsizing as their profits climb. "All things being equal, we'd be better off spreading around the work," observes labor economist Ronald G. Ehrenberg of Cornell University.

Yet a host of factors pushes employers to hire fewer workers for more hours and at the same time compels workers to spend more time on the job. Most of those incentives involve what Ehrenberg calls the structure of compensation: quirks in the way salaries and benefits are organized that make it more profitable to ask 40 employees to labor an extra hour each than to hire one more worker to do the same 40-hour job.

Professional and managerial employees supply the most obvious lesson along these lines. Once people are on salary, their cost to a firm is the same whether they spend 35 hours a week in the office or 70. Diminishing returns may eventually set in as overworked employees lose efficiency or leave for more arable pastures. But in the short run, the employer's incentive is clear. Even hourly employees receive benefits - such as pension contributions and medical insurance - that are not tied to the number of hours they work. Therefore, it is more profitable for employers to work their existing employees harder.

For all that employees complain about long hours, they too have reasons not to trade money for leisure. "People who work reduced hours pay a huge penalty in career terms," Schor maintains. "It's taken as a negative signal' about their commitment to the firm.' [Lotte] Bailyn [of Massachusetts Institute of Technology] adds that many corporate managers find it difficult to measure the contribution of their underlings to a firm's well-being, so they use the number of hours worked as a proxy for output. "Employees know this," she says, and they adjust their behavior accordingly.

"Although the image of the good worker is the one whose life belongs to the company," Bailyn says, "it doesn't fit the facts.' She cites both quantitative and qualitative studies that show increased productivity for part-time workers: they make better use of the time they have and they are less likely to succumb to fatigue in stressful jobs. Companies that employ more workers for less time also gain from the resulting redundancy, she asserts. "The extra people can cover the contingencies that you know are going to happen, such as when crises take people away from the workplace." Positive experiences with reduced hours have begun to change the more-is-better culture at some companies, Schor reports.

Larger firms, in particular, appear to be more willing to experiment with flexible working arrangements...

It may take even more than changes in the financial and cultural structures of employment for workers successfully to trade increased productivity and money for leisure time, Schor contends. She says the U.S. market for goods has become skewed by the assumption of full-time, two-career households. Automobile makers no longer manufacture cheap models, and developers do not build the tiny bungalows that served the first postwar generation of home buyers. Not even the humblest household object is made without a microprocessor. As Schor notes, the situation is a curious inversion of the "appropriate technology" vision that designers have had for developing countries: U.S. goods are appropriate only for high incomes and long hours. --- Paul Walluh.

Questions 27-32

Do the following statements agree with the views of the writer in reading passage 4? In boxes 27-32 on your answer sheet write:

YES   if the statement agrees with the writer
NO   if the statement contradicts the writer
NOT GIVEN if it is impossible to say what the writer thinks about this

Example	
	Answer
During the industrial revolution, people worked harder	NOT GIVEN

27 Today, employees are facing a reduction in working hours.
28 Social planners have been consulted about US employment figures.
29 Salaries have not risen significantly since the 1970s.
30 The economic recovery created more jobs.
31 Bailyn's research shows that part-time employees work more efficiently.
32 Increased leisure time would benefit two-career households.

Questions 33-34
choose the appropriate letters A-D and write them in boxes 33 and 34 on your answer sheet.

33 Bailyn argues that it is better for a company to employ more workers because
    A.   it is easy to make excess staff redundant.
    B.   crises occur if you are under-staffed.
    C.   people are available to substitute for absent staff.
    D.   they can project a positive image at work.

34 Schor thinks it will be difficult for workers in the US to reduce their working hours because
    A.   They would not be able to afford cars or homes.
    B.   employers are offering high incomes for long hours.
    C.   the future is dependent on technological advances.
    D.   they do not wish to return to the humble post-war era.

Questions 35-38
the writer mentions a number of factors that have resulted, in employees working longer hours. Which FOUR of the following factors are mentioned? Write your answers (A-H) in boxes 35-38 on your answer sheet.
List of Factors
A Books are available to help employees cope with stress.
B Extra work is offered to existing employees.
C Increased production has led to joblessness.
D Benefits and hours spent on the job are not linked.
E Overworked employees require longer to do their work.

F   Longer hours indicate a greater commitment to the firm.
G   Managers estimate staff productivity in terms of hours worked.
H   Employees value a career more than a family.

You should spend about 20 minutes on questions 1 to 13, which are best on reading passage 5 on the following pages.

MAKING EVERY DROP COUNT

A. The history of human civilization is entwined with the history of the ways we have learned to manipulate Water Resources. As towns gradually expanded, water was brought from increasingly remote sources, leading to sophisticated engineering efforts such as dams and Aqueducts. At the height of the Roman Empire, 9 major systems, with an Innovative layout of pipes and well- built sewers, supplied the occupants of Rome with as much water per person as is provided in many parts of the industrial world today.

B. During the Industrial Revolution and population explosion of the 19th and 20th centuries, the demons for water rose dramatically. Unprecedented construction of tens of thousands of monumental engineering projects designed to control floods, Project Clean Water Supplies, and provide water for irrigation and hydropower brought great benefits to hundreds of millions of people. Food production has kept pace with the soaring population mainly because of the expansion of artificial irrigation systems that make possible the growth of 40% of the world's food. Nearly one-fifth of all the electricity generated worldwide is produced by turbines spun by the power of falling water.

C. Yet there is a dark side to this picture: despite our progress, half of the world's population is still suffering; with water service inferior to those available to the ancient Greeks and Romans. As the United Nations report on access to water we reiterated in November 2001, more than 1 billion people lack access to clean drinking water; Some two and a half billion do not have adequate sanitation service. Preventable water-related deceased killed an estimated 10000 to 20,000 children every day, and the latest evidence suggests that we are falling behind in efforts to solve these problems.

D. The consequences of our water policies extend beyond jeopardizing human health. Tens of millions of people have been forced to move from their homes often with little warnings of compensation to make way for the reservoirs behind dams. More than 20% of all freshwater fish spices are now threatened or endangered because dams and Water Irrigation practices degrade soil quality and reduce agricultural productivity. Groundwater aquifers are being pumped down faster than they are naturally replenished in parts of India China the USA and elsewhere. And disputes over shared Water Resources have led to violence and continue to raise local, national, and even international tensions.

E. At the outset of the new millennium, however,   the way resource planners think water is beginning to change. The focus is slowly shifting back to the provision of basic human and environmental needs as a top priority ensuring "some for all" instead of more for some.   Some water experts are now demanding that existing infrastructure be used in smarter ways rather than building new facilities, which is increasingly considered the option of last, not First, Resort. This shift in philosophy has not been universally accepted, and it comes with strong opposition from some established water organizations. Nevertheless, it may be the only way to address successfully the pressing problems of providing everyone with clean water to drink, adequate water to grow food, and A life free from a preventable water-related illness.

F. Fortunately and unexpectedly the demand for water is not rising as rapidly as some predicted. As a result, the pressure to build new water infrastructures has diminished over the past two decades. Although population , industrial output, and economic productivity have continued to soar in developed Nation, the rate at which people withdraw water from aquifers, rivers, and lakes has slowed. And in a few parts of the world, demand has actual Fallen.

G. What explains this remarkable turn of events? : 2 factors: people have figured out how to use water more efficiently, and communities are rethinking their priorities for water use. Throughout the first three-quarters of the 20th century, the quality of freshwater consumed per person doubled on average; in the USA, water withdrawals increased tenfold while the population quadrupled. But since 1980, the amount of water consumed per person has actually decreased, thanks to a range of new technologies that helped to conserve water in homes and Industry. in 1965, for instance, Japan used approximately 30 million gallons of water to produce $1 million of the commercial output; but 1989 this had dropped to 3.5 million gallons(even accounting for inflation) almost quadrupling off water productivity. In the USA, water withdrawals have fallen by more than 20% from that peak in 1980.

H. On the other hand, dams, aqueducts, and other kinds of infrastructure will still have to be built, but such a project must be built to higher specifications and with more accountability to local people and their environment than in the past. And even in regions where new projects seem warranted, we must find ways to meet demands with fewer resources, respecting ecological criteria, and to a smaller budget.

Question 1 to 7

Reading passage 1 has 7 paragraph, A-H

Choose the correct heading for paragraph A and C-H from the list of heading below. Write the correct number i-xi, in boxes 1-7 on your answer sheet.

LIST OF HEADINGS

i   scientists call for a revision of policy

ii   i an explanation for reduced Water use

iii   i how a global challenge was met

iv   irrigation systems fall into disuse

v   environmental effects

Vi   the financial cost of recent technological improvements

Vii   the relevance to health

Viii   addressing the concern over increasing populations

ix   as surprising downward Trend in demand for water

X   the need to raise standards

Xi   a description of ancient Water Supplies

> Example
> Answer
> Paragraph B
> iii

1 Paragraph   A
2 Paragraph   C
3 Paragraph   D
4 Paragraph   E
5 Paragraph   F
6 Paragraph   G
7 Paragraph   H

Question 8 to 13

Do the following statements agree with the information given in the reading passage 1?

In boxes 18 to 13 on your answer sheet, write

YES   *if the statement agrees with the claims of the writer*

NO   *if statement contradicts the claims of the writer*

NOT GIVEN   *if the impossible to say what the writer thinks about this*

8 what are use Person is higher in the industrial world than it was in ancient Rome

9 feeding increasing populations is possible due primarily to improved irrigation systems

10 modern water systems imitate those of the ancient Greeks and Romans

11 industrial growth is increasing the overall demand for water

12 modern technology has helped led to a reduction in domestic water consumption

13 in the future, governments should maintain ownership of water infrastructures.

READING PASSAGE 06

You should spend about 20 minutes on Questions 1-13 which are based on Reading Passage 6 below.

A Remarkable Beetle

Some of the most remarkable beetles are the dung beetles, which spend almost their whole lives eating and breeding in dung'.

More than 4,000 species of these remarkable creatures have evolved and adapted to the world's different climates and the dung of its many animals. Australia's native dung beetles are scrub and woodland dwellers, specializing in coarse marsupial droppings and avoiding the soft cattle dung in which bush flies and buffalo flies breed.

In the early 1960s George Bornemissza, then a scientist at the Australian Government's premier research organization, the Commonwealth Scientific and Industrial Research Organization (CSIRO), suggested that dung beetles should be introduced to Australia to control dung-breeding flies. Between 1968 and 1982, the CSIRO imported insects from about 50 different species of dung beetle, from Asia, Europe and Africa, aiming to match them to different climatic zones in Australia. Of the 26 species that are known to have become successfully integrated into the local environment, only one, an African species released in northern Australia, has reached its natural boundary.

Introducing dung beetles into a pasture is a simple process: approximately 1,500 beetles are released; a handful at a time, into fresh cow pats 2 in the cow pasture. The beetles immediately disappear beneath the pats digging and tunneling and, if they successfully adapt to their new environment, soon become a permanent, self-sustaining part of the local ecology. In time they multiply and within three or four years the benefits to the pasture are obvious.

Dung beetles work from the inside of the pat so they are sheltered from predators such as birds and foxes. Most species burrow into the soil and bury dung in tunnels directly underneath the pats, which are hollowed out from within. Some large species originating from France excavate tunnels to a depth of approximately 30 cm below the dung pat. These beetles make sausage-shaped brood chambers along the tunnels. The shallowest tunnels belong to a much smaller Spanish species that buries dung in chambers that hang like fruit from the branches of a pear tree. South African beetles dig narrow tunnels of approximately 20 cm below the surface of the pat. Some surface-dwelling beetles, including a South African species, cut perfectly-shaped balls from the pat, which are rolled away and attached to the bases of plants.

For maximum dung burial in spring, summer and autumn, farmers require a variety of species with overlapping periods of activity. In the cooler environments of the state of Victoria, the large French species (2.5 cms long) is matched with smaller (half this size), temperate-climate Spanish species. The former are slow to recover from the winter cold and produce only one or two generations of offspring from late spring until autumn. The latter, which multiplies rapidly in early spring, produce two to five generations annually. The South African ball-rolling species, being a subtropical beetle, prefers the climate of northern and coastal New South Wales where it commonly works with the South African tunnelling species. In warmer climates, many species are active for longer periods of the year.

Dung beetles were initially introduced in the late 1960s with a view to controlling buffalo flies by removing the dung within a day or two and so preventing flies from breeding. However, other benefits have become evident. Once the beetle larvae have finished pupation, the residue is a first-rate source of fertilizer. The tunnels abandoned by the beetles provide excellent aeration and water channels for root systems. In addition, when the new generation of beetles has left the nest the abandoned burrows are an attractive habitat for soil-enriching earthworms. The digested dung in these burrows is an excellent food supply for the earthworms, which decompose it further to provide essential soil nutrients. If it were not for the dung beetle, chemical fertilizer and dung would be washed by rain into streams and rivers before it could be absorbed into the hard earth, polluting water courses and causing blooms of blue-green algae. Without the beetles to dispose of the dung, cow pats would litter pastures making grass inedible to cattle and depriving the soil of sunlight. Australia's 30 million cattle each produce 10-12 cow pats a day. This amounts to 1.7 billion tons a year, enough to smother about 110,000 sq km of pasture, half the area of Victoria.

Dung beetles have become an integral part of the successful management of dairy farms in Australia over the past few decades. A number of species are available from the CSIRO or through a small number of private breeders, most of whom were entomologists with the CSIRO's dung beetle unit who have taken their specialised knowledge of the insect and opened small businesses in direct competition with their former employer.

Glossary
1. dung:- the droppings or excreta of animals
2. cow pats:- droppings of cows

Questions 1-5
Do the following statements reflect the claims of the writer in Reading Passage 6? In boxes 1-5 on your answer sheet write:

    YES   if the statement reflects the claims of the writer
    NO   if the statement contradicts the claims of the writer
    NOT GIVEN if it is impossible to say what the writer thinks about this

1   Bush flies are easier to control than buffalo flies.
2   Four thousand species of dung beetle were initially brought to Australia by the CSIRO.
3   Dung beetles were brought to Australia by the CSIRO over a fourteen-year period.
4   At least twenty-six of the introduced species have become established in Australia.
5   The dung beetles cause an immediate improvement to the quality of a cow pasture.

Questions 6-8

Label the tunnels on the diagram below. Choose your labels from the box below the diagram. Write your answers in boxes 6-8 on your answer sheet.
Write your answers in boxes 6-8 on your answer sheet.

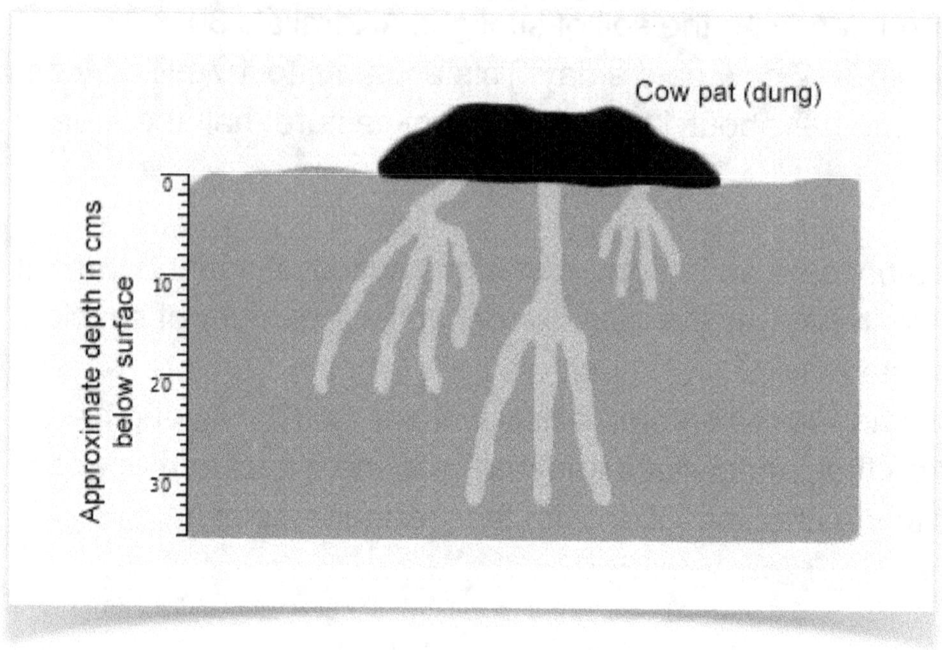

Dung Beetle Types	
French	Spanish
Mediterranean	South African
Australian native	South African ball roller.

Question 9-13

Complete the table below.

Choose NO MORE THAN THREE WORDS OR A NUMBER from Reading Passage 6 for each answer.

Write your answers in boxes 9—13 on your answer sheet.

Species	Size	Preferred Climate	Complementary species	Start of active period	Number of generations per year

French	2.5 cm	Cool	Spanish	Late spring	1-2
Spanish	1.2 5 cm	9		10	1
South African ball roller		12	13		

READING PASSAGE 07

You should spend about 20 minutes on Questions 1–14 which are based on Reading Passage Sample 7 below:
Alarming Rate of Loss of Tropical Rainforests

Adults and children are frequently confronted with statements about the

alarming rate of loss of tropical rainforests. For example, one graphic illustration to which children might readily relate is the estimate that rainforests are being destroyed at a rate equivalent to one thousand football fields every forty minutes – about the duration of a normal classroom period. In the face of the frequent and often vivid media coverage, it is likely that children will have formed ideas about rainforests – what and where they are, why they are important, what endangers them – independent of any formal tuition. It is also possible that some of these ideas will be mistaken. Many studies have shown that children harbor misconceptions about 'pure', curriculum science. These misconceptions do not remain isolated but become incorporated into a multifaceted, but organized, conceptual framework, making it and the component ideas, some of which are erroneous, more robust but also accessible to modification. These ideas may be developed by children absorbing ideas through the popular media. Sometimes this information may be erroneous. It seems schools may not be providing an opportunity for children to re-express their ideas and so have them tested and refined by teachers and their peers.

Despite the extensive coverage in the popular media of the destruction of rainforests, little formal information is available about children's ideas in this area. The aim of the present study is to start to provide such information, to help teachers design their educational strategies to build upon correct ideas and to displace misconceptions and to plan programmes in environmental studies in their schools.

The study surveys children's scientific knowledge and attitudes to rainforests. Secondary school children were asked to complete a questionnaire containing five open-form questions. The most frequent responses to the first question were descriptions which are self-evident from the term 'rainforest'. Some children described them as damp, wet or hot. The second question concerned the geographical location of rainforests. The commonest responses were continents or countries: Africa (given by 43% of children), South America (30%), Brazil (25%). Some children also gave more general locations, such as being near the Equator.

Responses to question three concerned the importance of rainforests. The dominant idea, raised by 64% of the pupils, was that rainforests provide animals with habitats. Fewer students responded that rainforests provide plant habitats, and even fewer mentioned the indigenous populations of rainforests. More girls (70%) than boys (60%) raised the idea of the rainforest as animal habitats.

Similarly, but at a lower level, more girls (13%) than boys (5%) said that rainforests provided human habitats. These observations are generally consistent with our previous studies of pupils' views about the use and conservation of rainforests, in which girls were shown to be more sympathetic to animals and expressed views which seem to place an intrinsic value on non-human animal life.

The fourth question concerned the causes of the destruction of rainforests. Perhaps encouragingly, more than half of the pupils (59%) identified that it is human activities which are destroying rainforests, some personalizing the responsibility by the use of terms such as 'we are'. About 18% of the pupils referred specifically to logging activity.

One misconception, expressed by some 10% of the pupils, was that acid rain is responsible for rainforest destruction; a similar proportion said that pollution is destroying rainforests. Here, children are confusing rainforest destruction with damage to the forests of Western Europe by these factors. While two-fifths of the students provided the information that the rainforests provide oxygen, in some cases this response also embraced the misconception that rainforest destruction would reduce atmospheric oxygen, making the atmosphere incompatible with human life on Earth.

In answer to the final question about the importance of rainforest conservation, the majority of children simply said that we need rainforests to survive. Only a few of the pupils (6%) mentioned that rainforest destruction may contribute to global warming. This is surprising considering the high level of media coverage on this issue. Some children expressed the idea that the conservation of rainforests is not important.

The results of this study suggest that certain ideas predominate in the thinking of children about rainforests. Pupils' responses indicate some misconceptions in the basic scientific knowledge of rainforest's ecosystems such as their ideas about rainforests as habitats for animals, plants and humans and the relationship between climatic change and destruction of rainforests.

Pupils did not volunteer ideas that suggested that they appreciated the complexity of causes of rainforest destruction. In other words, they gave no indication of an appreciation of either the range of ways in which rainforests are important or the complex social, economic and political factors which drive the activities which are destroying the rainforests. One encouragement is that the results of similar studies about other environmental issues suggest that older children seem to acquire the ability to appreciate, value and evaluate conflicting views. Environmental education offers an arena in which these skills can be developed, which is essential for these children as future decision-makers.

Questions 1–8

Do the following statements agree with the information given in Reading Sample 7?

In boxes 1–8 on your answer sheet write:

TRUE *if the statement agrees with the information*
FALSE *if the statement contradicts the information*
NOT GIVEN *if there is no information on this*

1 The plight of the rainforests has largely been ignored by the media.

2 Children only accept opinions on rainforests that they encounter in their classrooms.

3 It has been suggested that children hold mistaken views about the 'pure' science that they study at school.

4 The fact that children's ideas about science form part of a larger framework of ideas mean that it is easier to change them.

5 The study involved asking children a number of yes/no questions such as 'Are there any rainforests in Africa?'

6 Girls are more likely than boys to hold mistaken views about the rainforest's destruction.

7 The study reported here follows on from a series of studies that have looked at children's understanding of rainforests.

8 A second study has been planned to investigate primary school children's ideas about rainforests.

Questions 9–13

the box below gives a list of responses A–P to the questionnaire discussed in Reading sample 7.

Answer the following questions by choosing the correct responses A–P.

Write your answers in boxes 9–13 on your answer sheet.

09 What was the children's most frequent response when asked where the rainforests were?

10 What was the most common response to the question about the importance of the rainforests?

11 What did most children give as the reason for the loss of the rainforests?

12 Why did most children think it important for the rainforests to be protected?

13 Which of the responses is cited as unexpectedly uncommon, given the amount of time spent on the issue by the newspapers and television?

A There is a complicated combination of reasons for the loss of the rainforests.

B The rainforests are being destroyed by the same things that are destroying the forests of Western Europe.

C Rainforests are located near the Equator.

D Brazil is home to the rainforests.

E Without rainforests some animals would have nowhere to live.

F Rainforests are important habitats for a lot of plants.

G People are responsible for the loss of the rainforests.

H The rainforests are a source of oxygen.

I Rainforests are of consequence for a number of different reasons.

J As the rainforests are destroyed, the world gets warmer.

K Without rainforests there would not be enough oxygen in the air.

L   There are people for whom the rainforests are home.
M   Rainforests are found in Africa.
N   Rainforests are not really important to human life.
O   The destruction of the rainforests is the direct result of logging activity.
P   Humans depend on the rainforests for their continuing existence.

Question 14

Choose the correct letter A, B, C, D or E.

Write your answer in box 14 on your answer sheet.

Which of the following is the most suitable title for Reading sample Passage 7?

A The development of a program me in environmental studies within a science curriculum

B Children's ideas about the rainforests and the implications for course design

C The extent to which children have been misled by the media concerning the rainforests

D How to collect, collate and describe the ideas of secondary school children

E The importance of the rainforests and the reasons for their destruction

READING PASSAGE 08

You should spend about 20 minutes on Questions 14-27 which are based on Reading Passage sample 8 below.

Questions 14-18

Reading passage 8 has six paragraphs B-F from the list of headings below

Choose the most suitable headings for paragraphs B-F from the list of
headings below.
Write the appropriate numbers (i-ix) in boxes 14-18 on your answer sheet.

NB There are more headings than paragraphs, so you will not use them all.

List of Headings
i)   Ottawa International Conference on Health Promotion
ii)   Holistic approach to health
iii) The primary importance of environmental factors
iv)   Healthy lifestyles approach to health
v)   Changes in concepts of health in Western society
vi)   Prevention of diseases and illness
vii) Ottawa Charter for Health Promotion
viii) Definition of health in medical terms
 ix) Socio-ecological view of health

14.   Paragraph B
15.   Paragraph C
16.   Paragraph D
17.   Paragraph E
18.   Paragraph F

Changing Our Understanding of Health
A
The concept of health holds different meanings for different people and
groups. These meanings of health have also changed over time. This
change is no more evident than in Western society today, when notions of
health and health promotion are being challenged and expanded in new
ways.

B

For much of recent Western history, health has been viewed in the physical sense only. That is, good health has been connected to the smooth mechanical operation of the body, while ill health has been attributed to a breakdown in this machine. Health in this sense has been defined as the absence of disease or illness and is seen in medical terms. According to this view, creating health for people means providing medical care to treat or prevent disease and illness. During this period, there was an emphasis on providing clean water, improved sanitation and housing.

C

In the late 1940s the World Health Organization challenged this physically and medically oriented view of health. They stated that 'health is a complete state of physical, mental and social well-being and is not merely the absence of disease' (WHO, 1946). Health and the person were seen more holistically (mind/body/spirit) and not just in physical terms.

D

The 1970s was a time of focusing on the prevention of disease and illness by emphasizing the importance of the lifestyle and behavior of the individual. Specific behaviors which were seen to increase the risk of diseases, such as smoking, lack of fitness and unhealthy eating habits, were targeted. Creating health meant providing not only medical health care, but health promotion programs and policies which would help people maintain healthy behaviors and lifestyles. While this individualistic healthy lifestyle approach to health worked for some (the wealthy members of society), people experiencing poverty, unemployment, underemployment or little control over the conditions of their daily lives benefited little from this approach. This was largely because both the healthy lifestyles approach and the medical approach to health largely ignored the social and environmental conditions affecting the health of people.

E

During 1980s and 1990s there has been a growing swing away from seeing lifestyle risks as the root cause of poor health. While lifestyle factors still remain important, health is being viewed also in terms of the social, economic and environmental contexts in which people live. This broad approach to health is called the socio-ecological view of health. The broad socio-ecological view of health was endorsed at the first International Conference of Health Promotion held in 1986, Ottawa, and Canada, where people from 38 countries agreed and declared that:

The fundamental conditions and resources for health are peace, shelter, education, food, a viable income, a stable eco-system, sustainable resources, social justice and equity. Improvement in health requires a secure foundation in these basic requirements. (WHO, 1986).

It is clear from this statement that the creation of health is about much more than encouraging healthy individual behaviors and lifestyles and providing appropriate medical care. Therefore, the creation of health must include addressing issues such as poverty, pollution, urbanization, natural resource depletion, social alienation and poor working conditions. The social, economic and environmental contexts which contribute to the creation of health do not operate separately or independently of each other. Rather, they are interacting and interdependent, and it is the complex interrelationships between them which determine the conditions that promote health. A broad socio-ecological view of health suggests that the promotion of health must include a strong social, economic and environmental focus.

F

At the Ottawa Conference in 1986, a charter was developed which outlined new directions for health promotion based on the socio-ecological view of health. This charter, known as the Ottawa Charter for Health Promotion, remains as the backbone of health action today. In exploring the scope of health promotion it states that:

Good health is a major resource for social, economic and personal development and an important dimension of quality of life. Political, economic, social, cultural, environmental, behavioral and biological factors can all favor health or be harmful to it. (WHO, 1986) .

The Ottawa Charter brings practical meaning and action to this broad notion of health promotion. It presents fundamental strategies and approaches in achieving health for all. The overall philosophy of health promotion which guides these fundamental strategies and approaches is one of 'enabling people to increase control over and to improve their health' (WHO, 1986).

Questions 19-22
Using NO MORE THAN THREE WORDS from the passage, answer the following questions
write your answers in boxes 19-22 on your answer sheet.

19. In which year did the World Health Organization define health in terms of mental, physical and social well-being?
20. Which members of society benefited most from the healthy lifestyles approach to health?
21. Name the three broad areas which relate to people's health, according to the socio-ecological view of health.
22. During which decade were lifestyle risks seen as the major contributors to poor health?

Questions 23-27
Do the following statements agree with the information in Reading Passage 8?
In boxes 23-27 on your answer sheet write
      YES   if the statement agrees with the information.
      NO   if the statement contradicts the information.
      NOT GIVEN if there is no information on this in the passage.

23 Doctors have been instrumental in improving living standards in Western society.
24 The approach to health during the 1970s included the introduction of health awareness programs.
25 The socio-ecological view of health recognizes that lifestyle habits and

the provision of adequate health care are critical factors governing health.
26 The principles of the Ottawa Charter are considered to be out of date in
the 1990s.
27 In recent years a number of additional countries have subscribed to the
Ottawa Charter.

READING PASSAGE 09

You should spend about 20 minutes on Questions 30-41 which are based
on the Reading Passage below.

PAPER RECYCLING

A Paper is different from other waste produce because it comes from a
sustainable resource: trees. Unlike the minerals and oil used to make
plastics and metals, trees are replaceable. Paper is also biodegradable, so
it does not pose as much threat to the environment when it is discarded.
While 45 out of every 100 tons of wood fiber used to make paper in
Australia comes from waste paper, the rest comes directly from virgin fiber
from forests and plantations. By world standards, this is a good
performance since the worldwide average is 33 percent waste paper.
Governments have encouraged waste paper collection and sorting
schemes and at the same time, the paper industry has responded by
developing new recycling technologies that have paved the way for even
greater utilization of used fibre. As a result, industry's use of recycled fibres
is expected to increase at twice the rate of virgin fibre over the coming
years.
B Already, waste paper constitutes 70% of paper used for packaging and
advances in the technology required to remove ink from the paper have
allowed a higher recycled content in newsprint and writing paper. To

achieve the benefits of recycling, the community must also contribute. We need to accept a change in the quality of paper products; for example, stationery may be less white and of a rougher texture. There also needs to support from the community for waste paper collection programs. Not only do we need to make the paper available to collectors but it also needs to be separated into different types and sorted from contaminants such as staples, paperclips, string and other miscellaneous items.

C There are technical limitations to the amount of paper which can be recycled and some paper products cannot be collected for re-use. These include paper in the form of books and permanent records, photographic paper and paper which is badly contaminated. The four most common sources of paper for recycling are factories and retail stores which gather large amounts of packaging material in which goods are delivered, also offices which have unwanted business documents and computer output, paper converters and printers and lastly households which discard newspapers and packaging material. The paper manufacturer pays a price for the paper and may also incur the collection cost.

D Once collected, the paper has to be sorted by hand by people trained to recognize various types of paper. This is necessary because some types of paper can only be made from particular kinds of recycled fibre. The sorted paper then has to be repulsed or mixed with water and broken down into its individual fibres. This mixture is called stock and may contain a wide variety of contaminating materials, particularly if it is made from mixed waste paper which has had little sorting. Various machineries are used to remove other materials from the stock. After passing through the repulsing process, the fibres from printed waste paper are grey in colour because the printing ink has soaked into the individual fibres. This recycled material can only be used in products where the grey color does not matter, such as cardboard boxes but if the grey colour is not acceptable, the fibres must be de-inked. This involves adding chemicals such as caustic soda or other alkalis, soaps and detergents, water-hardening agents such as calcium chloride, frothing agents and bleaching agents. Before the recycled fibres can be made into paper they must be refined or treated in such a way that they bond together.

E Most paper products must contain some virgin fibre as well as recycled fibres and unlike glass, paper cannot be recycled indefinitely. Most paper is down-cycled which means that a product made from recycled paper is of an inferior quality to the original paper. Recycling paper is beneficial in that it saves some of the energy, labor and capital that go into producing virgin pulp. However, recycling requires the use of fossil fuel, a non-renewable energy source, to collect the waste paper from the community and to process it to produce new paper. And the recycling process still creates emissions which require treatment before they can be disposed of safely. Nevertheless, paper recycling is an important economic and environmental practice but one which must be carried out in a rational and viable manner for it to be useful to both industry and the community.

Questions 30-36

complete the summary below of the first two paragraphs of the Reading Passage.

Choose *ONE OR TWO WORDS* from the Reading Passage for each answer.

Write your answers in boxes 30-36 on your answer sheet.

SUMMARY

Example....

From the point of view of recycling, paper has two advantages over minerals and ....oil..........

in that firstly it comes from a resource which is .... (30) .... and secondly, it is less threatening to our environment when we throw it away because it is .... (31) ...... Although Australia's record in the re-use of waste paper is good, it is still necessary to use a combination of recycled fibre and .... (32) .... to make new paper. The paper industry has contributed positively and people have also been encouraged by .... (33) .... to collect their waste on a regular basis. One major difficulty is the removal of ink from used paper but .... (34) .... are being made in this area. However, we need to learn to accept paper which is generally of a lower .... (35) .... than before and to sort our waste paper by removing .... (36) .... before discarding it for collection.

Look at paragraphs C, D, and E and, using the information in the passage, complete the flow chart below. Write your answers in boxes 37-41 on your answer sheet. Use *ONE OR TWO WORDS* for each answer.

Waste Paper collected from:
Factories
Retail stores
(37)..............................
paper converted and printers
Households

The Paper is then
(38)...

↓

and

(39) ....
by adding water

↓

Chemicals are added in order to
(40) ....

The fibres are then
(41) ....

←

READING PASSAGE 10

You should spend about 20 minutes on Questions 1-13 which are based on Reading Passage 10 below.

ABSENTEEISM IN NURSING: A LONGITUDINAL STUDY
Absence from work is a costly and disruptive problem for any organization. The cost of absenteeism in Australia has been put at 1.8 million hours per day or $1400 million annually. The study reported here was conducted in the Prince William Hospital in Brisbane, Australia, where, prior to this time, few active steps had been taken to measure, understand or manage the occurrence of absenteeism.

Nursing Absenteeism

A prevalent attitude amongst many nurses in the group selected for study was that there was no reward or recognition for not utilizing the paid sick leave entitlement allowed them in their employment conditions. Therefore, they believed they may as well take the days off — sick or otherwise. Similar attitudes have been noted by *James (1989)*, who noted that sick leave is seen by many workers as a right, like annual holiday leave. *Miller and Norton (1986)*, in their survey of 865 nursing personnel, found that 73 percent felt they should be rewarded for not taking sick leave because some employees always used their sick leave. Further, 67 per cent of nurses felt that administration was not sympathetic to the problems shift work causes to employees' personal and social lives. Only 53 percent of the respondents felt that every effort was made to schedule staff fairly. In another longitudinal study of nurses working in two Canadian hospitals, *Hacket Bycio and Guion (1989)* examined the reasons why nurses took absence from work. The most frequent reason stated for absence was minor illness to self. Other causes, in decreasing order of frequency, were illness in family, family social function, work to do at home and bereavement.

Method

In an attempt to reduce the level of absenteeism amongst the 250 registered an Enrolled Nurses in the present study, the Prince William management introduced three different, yet potentially complementary, strategies over 18 months. *Strategy 1: Non-financial (material) incentives:* Within the established wage and salary system it was not possible to use hospital funds to support this strategy. However, it was possible to secure incentives from local businesses, including free passes to entertainment parks, theatres, restaurants, etc. At the end of each roster period, the ward with the lowest absence rate would win the prize. *Strategy 2 Flexible fair roistering:* Where possible, staff were given the opportunity to determine their working schedule within the limits of clinical needs. *Strategy 3: Individual absenteeism :* and Each month, managers would analyses the pattern of absence of staff with excessive sick leave (greater than ten days per year for full-time employees). Characteristic patterns of potential 'voluntary absenteeism' such as absence before and after days off, excessive weekend and night duty absence and multiple single days off were communicated to all ward nurses and then, as necessary, followed up by action.

Results

Absence rates for the six months prior to the Incentive scheme ranged from 3.69 per cent to 4.32 per cent. In the following six months, they ranged between 2.87 percent and 3.96 percent. This represents a 20 percent improvement. However, analysing the absence rates on a year-to-year basis, the overall absence rate was 3.60 percent in the first year and 3.43 percent in the following year. This represents a 5 percent decrease from the first to the second year of the study. A significant decrease in absence over the two-year period could not be demonstrated.

Discussion

The non-financial incentive scheme did appear to assist in controlling absenteeism in the short term. As the scheme progressed it became harder to secure prizes and this contributed to the program's losing momentum and finally ceasing. There were mixed results across wards as well. For example, in wards with staff members who had a long-term genuine illness, there was little chance of winning, and to some extent, the staffs on those wards were disempowered. Our experience would suggest that the long-term effects of incentive awards on absenteeism are questionable.

Over the time of the study, staff were given a larger degree of control in their rosters. This led to significant improvements in communication between managers and staff. A similar effect was found from the implementation of the third strategy. Many of the nurses had not realised the impact their behaviour was having on the organisation and their colleagues but there were also staff members who felt that talking to them about their absenteeism was 'picking' on them and this usually had a negative effect on management—employee relationships.

Conclusion

Although there has been some decrease in absence rates, no single strategy or combination of strategies has had a significant impact on absenteeism per se. Notwithstanding the disappointing results, it is our contention that the strategies were not in vain. A shared ownership of absenteeism and a collaborative approach to problem solving has facilitated improved cooperation and communication between management and staff. It is our belief that this improvement alone, while not tangibly measurable, has increased the ability of management to manage the effects of absenteeism more effectively since this study.

[" This article has been adapted and condensed from the article by G. William and K. Slater (1996), 'Absenteeism in nursing: A longitudinal study', Asia Pacific Journal of Human Resources, 34(1): 111-21. Names and other details have been changed and report findings may have been given a different emphasis from the original. We are grateful to the authors and Asia Pacific Journal of Human Resources for allowing us to use the material in this way. "]

Questions 1-7

Do the following statements agree with the information given in Reading Passage.

In boxes 1-7 on your answer sheet write:

YES   if the statement agrees with the information
NO   if the statement contradicts the information
NOT GIVEN if there is no information on this in the passage

1. The Prince William Hospital has been trying to reduce absenteeism amongst nurses for many years.

2. Nurses in the Prince William Hospital study believed that there were benefits in taking as little sick leave as possible.

3. Just over half the nurses in the 1986 study believed that management understood the effects that shift work had on them.

4. The Canadian study found that 'illness in the family' was a greater cause of absenteeism than 'work to do at home'.

5. In relation to management attitude to absenteeism the study at the Prince William Hospital found similar results to the two 1989 studies.

6. The study at the Prince William Hospital aimed to find out the causes of absenteeism amongst 250 nurses.

7. The study at the Prince William Hospital involved changes in management practices.

Questions 8-13

Complete the notes below.

Choose ONE OR TWO WORDS from the passage, for each answer.

Write your answers in boxes 8-13 on your answer sheet.

In the first strategy, wards with the lowest absenteeism in different periods would win prizes donated by .... (8) ....
In the second strategy, staff were given more control over their ......(9)........
In the third strategy, nurses who appeared to be taking ...... (10)...... sick leave or ...... (11) ...... were identified and counselled.
Initially, there was a ...... (12)...... per cent decrease in absenteeism.
The first strategy was considered ineffective and stopped.
The second and third strategies generally resulted in better ......
(13) ...... among staff.

READING PASSAGE 11

You should spend about 20 minutes on Questions 1-14, which are based on the following reading passage:

THE ROCKET - FROM EAST TO WEST

A The concept of the rocket, or rather the mechanism behind the idea of propelling an object into the air, has been around for well over two thousand years. However, it wasn't until the discovery of the reaction principle, which was the key to space travel and so represents one of the great milestones in the history of scientific thought, that rocket technology was able to develop. Not only did it solve a problem that had intrigued man for ages, but, more importantly, it literally opened the door to the exploration of the universe.

B An intellectual breakthrough, brilliant though it may be, does not automatically ensure that the transition is made from theory to practice. Despite the fact that rockets had been used sporadically for several hundred years, they remained a relatively minor artefact of civilization until the twentieth century. Prodigious efforts, accelerated during two world wars, were required before the technology of primitive rocketry could be translated into the reality of sophisticated astronauts. It is strange that the rocket was generally ignored by writers of fiction to transport their heroes to mysterious realms beyond the Earth, even though it had been commonly used in fireworks displays in China since the thirteenth century. The reason is that nobody associated the reaction principle with the idea of traveling through space to a neighbouring world.

C A simple analogy can help us to understand how a rocket operates. It is much like a machine gun mounted on the rear of a boat. In reaction to the backward discharge of bullets, the gun, and hence the boat, move forwards. A rocket motor's 'bullets' are minute, high-speed particles produced by burning propellants in a suitable chamber. The reaction to the ejection of these small particles causes the rocket to move forwards. There is evidence that the reaction principle was applied practically well before the rocket was invented. In his Noctes Atticae or Greek Nights, Aulus Gellius describes 'the pigeon of Archytas', an invention dating back to about 360 BC. Cylindrical in shape, made of wood, and hanging from string, it was moved to and fro by steam blowing out from small exhaust ports at either end. The reaction to the discharging steam provided the bird with motive power.

D The invention of rockets is linked inextricably with the invention of 'black powder'. Most historians of technology credit the Chinese with its discovery. They base their belief on studies of Chinese writings or on the notebooks of early Europeans who settled in or made long visits to China to study its history and civilisation. It is probable that, sometime in the tenth century, black powder was first compounded from its basic ingredients of saltpetre, charcoal and sulphur. But this does not mean that it was immediately used to propel rockets. By the thirteenth century, powder propelled fire arrows had become rather common. The Chinese relied on this type of technological development to produce incendiary projectiles of many sorts, explosive grenades and possibly cannons to repel their enemies. One such weapon was the 'basket of fire' or, as directly translated from Chinese, the 'arrows like flying leopards'. The 0.7 metre-long arrows, each with a long tube of gunpowder attached near the point of each arrow, could be fired from a long, octagonal-shaped basket at the same time and had a range of 400 paces. Another weapon was the 'arrow as am flying sabre', which could be fired from crossbows. The rocket, placed in a similar position to other rocket-propelled arrows, was designed to increase the range. A small iron weight was attached to the 1.5m bamboo shaft, just below the feathers, to increase the arrow's stability by moving the centre of gravity to a position below the rocket. At a similar time, the Arabs had developed the 'egg which moves and burns'. This 'egg' was apparently full of gunpowder and stabilised by a 1.5m tail. It was fired using two rockets attached to either side of this tail.

E It was not until the eighteenth century that Europe became seriously interested in the possibilities of using the rocket itself as a weapon of war and not just to propel other weapons. Prior to this, rockets were used only in pyrotechnic displays. The incentive for the more aggressive use of rockets came not from within the European continent but from far-away India, whose leaders had built up a corps of rocketeers and used rockets successfully against the British in the late eighteenth century. The Indian rockets used against the British were described by a British Captain serving in India as 'an iron envelope about 200 millimetres long and 40 millimetres in diameter with sharp points at the top and a 3m-long bamboo guiding stick'. In the early nineteenth century, the British began to experiment with incendiary barrage rockets. The British rocket differed from the Indian version in that it was completely encased in a stout, iron cylinder, terminating in a conical head, measuring one metre in diameter and having a stick almost five metres long and constructed in such a way that it could be firmly attached to the body of the rocket. The Americans developed a rocket, complete with its own launcher, to use against the Mexicans in the mid-nineteenth century. A long cylindrical tube was propped up by two sticks and fastened to the top of the launcher, thereby allowing the rockets to be inserted and lit from the other end. However, the results were sometimes not that impressive as the behaviour of the rockets in flight was less than predictable. Since then, there have been huge developments in rocket technology, often with devastating results in the forum of war. Nevertheless, the modern day space programs owe their success to the humble beginnings of those in previous centuries who developed the foundations of the reaction principle. Who knows what it will be like in the future?

Questions 1-4
Reading passage 11 has six paragraphs labelled A-F.
Choose the most suitable headings for paragraphs B-E from the list of headings below.
Write the appropriate numbers (i-ix) in boxes 1-4 on your answer sheet.

List of Headings

i   How the reaction principle works
ii   The impact of the reaction principle
iii Writer's theories of the reaction principle
iv   Undeveloped for centuries
v   The first rockets
vi   The first use of steam
vii Rockets for military use
viii Developments of fire
ix   What's next?

Example   Paragraph A   Answer ii

1. Paragraph B
2. Paragraph C
3. Paragraph D
4. Paragraph E

Questions 5 and 6
Choose the appropriate letters A-D and write them in boxes 5 and 6 on your answer sheet.

5 The greatest outcome of the discovery of the reaction principle was that

A   rockets could be propelled into the air.
B   space travel became a reality.
C   a major problem had been solved.
D   bigger rockets were able to be built.

6 According to the text, the greatest progress in rocket technology was made
A   from the tenth to the thirteenth centuries.
B   from the seventeenth to the nineteenth centuries.
C   from the early nineteenth to the late nineteenth century.
D   from the late nineteenth century to the present day.

Questions 7-10
From the information in the text, indicate who FIRST invented or used the items in the list below.
Write the appropriate letters A-E in boxes 7-10 on your answer sheet.
NB You may use any letter more than once.

Example   A
nswer
rockets for displays
A

7 black powder
8 rocket-propelled arrows for fighting
9 rockets as war weapons
10 the rocket launcher

FIRST invented or used by
A the Chinese
B the Indians
C the British
D the Arabs
E the Americans

Questions 11-14
Look at the drawings of different projectiles below, A-H, and the names of

*types of projectiles given
in the passage, Questions 11-14. Match each name with one drawing.
Write the appropriate letters A-H in boxes 11-14 on your answer sheet.*

Example   Answer
The Greek 'pigeon of Archytas'   C

11   The Chinese 'basket of fire'
12   The Arab 'egg which moves and burns'
13   The Indian rocket
14   The British barrage rocket

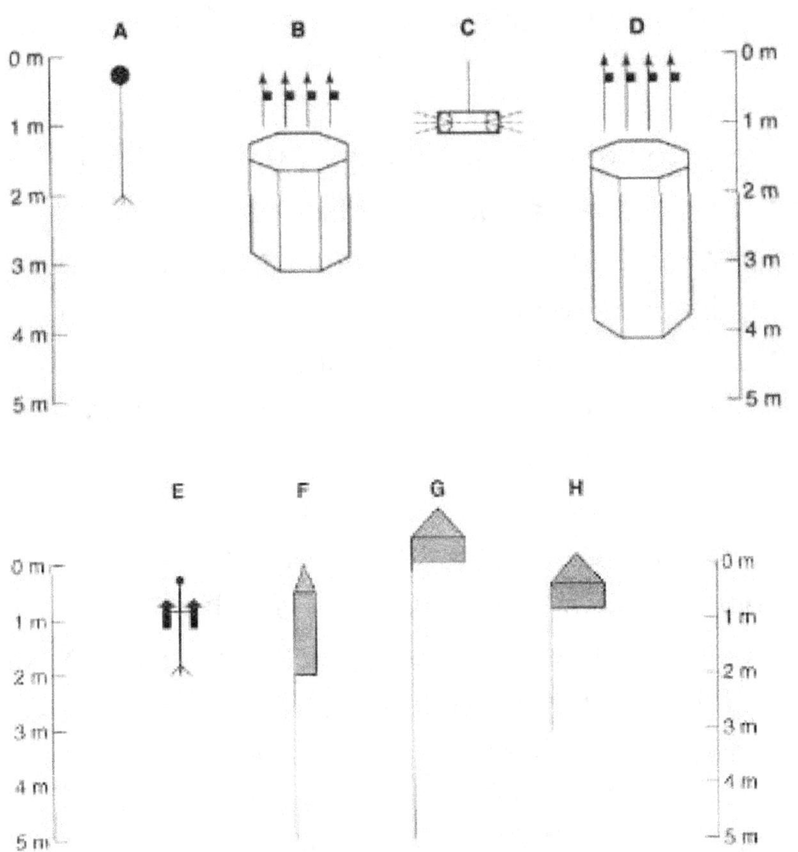

READING PASSAGE 12

You should spend about 20 minutes on Questions 29-40 which are based on the Reading Passage below.

THE SCIENTIFIC METHOD

A 'Hypotheses,' said Medawar in 1964, are imaginative and inspirational in character'; they are 'adventures of the mind'. He was arguing in favour of the position taken by Karl Popper in The Logic of Scientific Discovery (1972, 3rd edition) that the nature of scientific method is hypothetico-deductive and not, as is generally believed, inductive.

B It is essential that you, as an intending researcher, understand the difference between these two interpretations of the research process so that you do not become discouraged or begin to suffer from a feeling of 'cheating' or not going about it the right way.

C The myth of scientific method is that it is inductive: that the formulation of scientific theory starts with the basic, raw evidence of the senses - simple, unbiased, unprejudiced observation. Out of these sensory data - commonly referred to as 'facts' — generalisations will form. The myth is that from a disorderly array of factual information an orderly, relevant theory will somehow emerge. However, the starting point of induction is an impossible one.

D There is no such thing as an unbiased observation. Every act of observation we make is a function of what we have seen or otherwise experienced in the past. All scientific work of an experimental or exploratory nature starts with some expectation about the outcome. This expectation is a hypothesis. Hypotheses provide the initiative and incentive for the inquiry and influence the method. It is in the light of an expectation that some observations are held to be relevant and some irrelevant, that one methodology is chosen and others discarded, that some experiments are conducted and others are not. Where is, your naive, pure and objective researcher now?

E Hypotheses arise by guesswork, or by inspiration, but having been formulated they can and must be tested rigorously, using the appropriate methodology. If the predictions you make as a result of deducing certain consequences from your hypothesis are not shown to be correct then you discard or modify your hypothesis.If the predictions turn out to be correct then your hypothesis has been supported and may be retained until such time as some further test shows it not to be correct. Once you have arrived at your hypothesis, which is a product of your imagination, you then proceed to a strictly logical and rigorous process, based upon deductive argument — hence the term 'hypothetico-deductive'.

F So don't worry if you have some idea of what your results will tell you before you even begin to collect data; there are no scientists in existence who really wait until they have all the evidence in front of them before they try to work out what it might possibly mean. The closest we ever get to this situation is when something happens by accident; but even then the researcher has to formulate a hypothesis to be tested before being sure that, for example, a mould might prove to be a successful antidote to bacterial infection.

G The myth of scientific method is not only that it is inductive (which we have seen is incorrect) but also that the hypothetico-deductive method proceeds in a step-by-step, inevitable fashion. The hypothetico-deductive method describes the logical approach to much research work, but it does not describe the psychological behaviour that brings it about. This is much more holistic — involving guesses, reworkings, corrections, blind alleys and above all inspiration, in the deductive as well as the hypothetic component -than is immediately apparent from reading the final thesis or published papers. These have been, quite properly, organised into a more serial, logical order so that the worth of the output may be evaluated independently of the behavioural processes by which it was obtained. It is the difference, for example between the academic papers with which Crick and Watson demonstrated the structure of the DNA molecule and the fascinating book The Double Helix in which Watson (1968) described how they did it. From this point of view, 'scientific method' may more usefully be thought of as a way of writing up research rather than as a way of carrying it out.

Questions 29-30

Reading Passage 12 has seven paragraphs A-G.

Choose the most suitable headings for paragraphs C-G from the list of headings below.

Write the appropriate numbers i-x in boxes 29-33 on your answer sheet.

List of Headings

i	The Crick and Watson approach to research
ii	Antidotes to bacterial infection
iii	The testing of hypotheses
iv	Explaining the inductive method
v	Anticipating results before data is collected
vi	How research is done and how it is reported
vii	The role of hypotheses in scientific research
viii	Deducing the consequences of hypotheses
ix	Karl Popper's claim that the scientific method is hypothetico-deductive
x	The unbiased researcher

Example   Paragraph A   Answer: ix

29   Paragraph C

30   Paragraph D

31   Paragraph E

32   Paragraph
          F

33   Paragraph G

Questions 34 and 35
In which TWO paragraphs in Reading Passage12 does the writer give
advice directly to the reader?
Write the TWO appropriate letters (A—G) in boxes 34 and 35 on your
answer sheet.
Questions 36-39
Do the following statements reflect the opinions of the writer in Reading
Passage 12?
In boxes 36-39 on your answer sheet write
YES if the statement reflects the opinion of the writer.
NO if the statement contradicts the opinion of the writer.
NOT GIVEN if it is impossible to say what the writer thinks about this
36 Popper says that the scientific method is hypothetico-deductive.
37 If a prediction based on a hypothesis is fulfilled, then the hypothesis is
confirmed as true.
38 Many people carry out research in a mistaken way.
39 The 'scientific method' is more a way of describing research than a way
of doing it.

Question 40
Choose the appropriate letter A-D and write it in box 40 on your answer
sheet.
Which of the following statements best describes the writer's main purpose
in Reading Passage 3?
A to advise Ph.D students not to cheat while carrying out research.
B to encourage Ph.D students to work by guesswork and inspiration.
C to explain to Ph.D students the logic which the scientific research paper

follows.
D to help Ph.D students by explaining different conceptions of the research process.
READING PASSAGE 13

You are advised to spend about 20 minutes on Questions 27 - 40.
A.D.D. - Missing Out on Learning
Study requires a student's undivided attention. It is impossible to acquire a complex skill or absorb information about a subject in class unless one learns to concentrate without undue stress for long periods of time.

Students with Attention Deficit Disorder (A.D.D.) are particularly deficient in this respect for reasons which are now known to be microbiological and not behavioral, as was once believed. Of course, being unable to concentrate, and incapable of pleasing the teacher and oneself in the process, quickly leads to despondence and low self-esteem. This will naturally induce behavioral problems. It is estimated that 3 - 5 % of all children suffer from Attention Deficit Disorder. There are three main types of Attention Deficit Disorder: A.D.D. without Hyperactivity, A.D.D. with Hyperactivity (A.D.H.D.), and Undifferentiated A.D.D.

The characteristics of a person with A.D.D. are as follows:
• has difficulty paying attention
• does not appear to listen
• is unable to carry out given instructions
• avoids or dislikes tasks which require sustained mental effort
• has difficulty with organization
• is easily distracted
• often loses things
• is forgetful in daily activities

Children with A.D.H.D. also exhibit excessive and inappropriate physical activity, such as constant fidgeting and running about the room. This boisterousness often interferes with the educational development of others. Undifferentiated A.D.D. sufferers exhibit some, but not all, of the symptoms of each category.

It is important to base remedial action on an accurate diagnosis. Since A.D.D. is a physiological disorder caused by some structural or chemically-based neurotransmitter problem in the nervous system, it responds especially well to certain psycho stimulant drugs, such as Ritalin. In use since 1953, the drug enhances the ability to structure and complete a thought without being overwhelmed by non-related and distracting thought processes.

Psycho stimulants are the most widely used medications for persons with A.D.D. and A.D.H.D. Recent findings have validated the use of stimulant medications, which work in about 70 - 80% of A.H.D.D. children and adults (Wilens and Biederman, 1997). In fact, up to 90% of destructibility in A.D.D. sufferers can be removed by medication. The specific dose of medicine varies for each child, but such drugs are not without side effects, which include reduction in appetite, loss of weight, and problems with falling asleep.

Not all students who are inattentive in class have Attention Deficit Disorder. Many are simply unwilling to commit themselves to the task at hand. Others might have a specific learning disability (S.L.D.). However, those with A.D.D. have difficulty performing in school not usually because they have trouble learning 1 , but because of poor organization, inattention, compulsion and impulsiveness. This is brought about by an incompletely understood phenomenon, in which the individual is, perhaps, best described as 'tuning out' for short to long periods of time. The effect is analogous to the switching of channels on a television set. The difference is that an A.D.D. sufferer is not 'in charge of the remote control'. The child with A.D.D. is unavailable to learn - something else has involuntarily captured his or her whole attention.

It is commonly thought that A.D.D. only affects children, and that they grow out of the condition once they reach adolescence. It is now known that this is often not the case. Left undiagnosed or untreated, children with all forms of A.D.D. risk a lifetime of failure to relate effectively to others at home, school, college and at work. This brings significant emotional disturbances into play, and is very likely to negatively affect self-esteem. Fortunately, early identification of the problem, together with appropriate treatment, makes it possible for many victims to overcome the substantial obstacles that A.D.D. places in the way of successful learning.

1 approximately 15% of A.D.H.D. children do, however, have learning disabilities

Alternative Treatments for A.D.D.	Evaluation
<ul><li>EEG Biofeedback</li><li>Dietary intervention (*removal of food additives -preservatives, colorings etc.*)</li><li>Sugar reduction (in A.D.H.D.)</li><li>Correction of (supposed) inner-ear disturbance</li><li>Correction of (supposed) yeast infection (Candida albicans)</li><li>Vitamin/mineral regimen for (supposed) genetic abnormality</li><li>Body manipulations for (supposed) misalignment of two bones in the skull</li></ul>	<ul><li>expensive</li><li>trials flawed - (sample groups small, no control groups)</li><li>ineffective</li><li>numerous studies disprove link.</li><li>slightly effective (but only for a small percentage of children)</li><li>undocumented, unscientific studies</li><li>inconsistent with current theory</li><li>lack of evidence</li><li>inconsistent with current theory</li><li>lack of evidence</li><li>theory disproved in the 1970s</li><li>lack of evidence</li><li>inconsistent with current</li></ul>

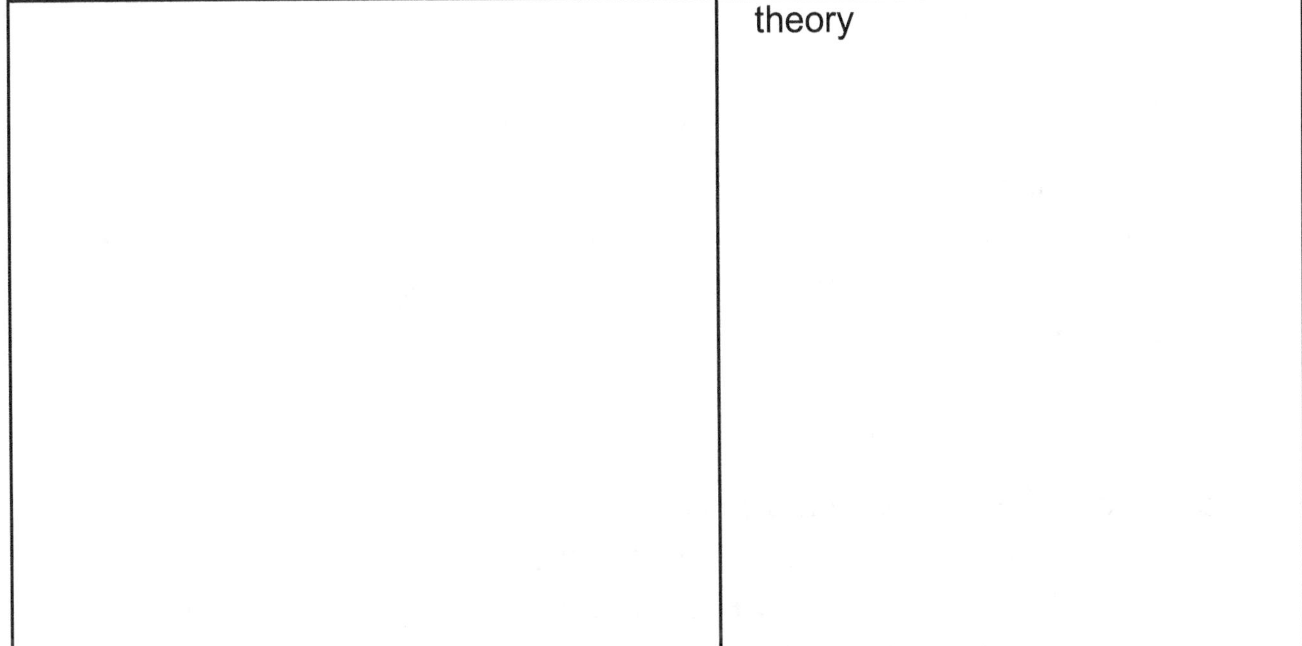

Figure 1. Evaluations of Controversial Treatments for A.D.D.

Questions 27-29
You are advised to spend about 5 minutes on Questions 27-29.

Refer to Reading Passage 13 "A.D.D. - Missing Out On Learning", and decide which of the answers best completes the following sentences. Write your answers in boxes 27 - 29 on your Answer Sheet. The first one has been done for you as an example.

Example: The number of main types of A.D.D. is:
a) 1
b) 2
c) 3
d) 4

Q. 27. Attention Deficit Disorder:

a) is a cause of behavioural problems
b) is very common in children
c) has difficulty paying attention

d) none of the above

Q. 28. Wilens and Biederman have shown that:

a) stimulant medications are useful
b) psychostimulants do not always work
c) hyperactive persons respond well to psychostimulants
d) all of the above

Q. 29. Children with A.D.D.:

a) have a specific learning disability
b) should not be given medication as a treatment
c) may be slightly affected by sugar intake
d) usually improve once they become teenagers

Questions 30-37
You are advised to spend about 10 minutes on Questions 30 - 37.
The following is a summary of Reading Passage 13.

Complete each gap in the text by choosing 30 - 37 on your Answer Sheet.
Write your answers in boxes. Note that there are more choices in the box
than gaps.

You will not need to use all the choices given, but you may use a word, or phrase more than once.

Attention Deficit Disorder is a neurobiological problem that affects 3 - 5% of all .....(Ex:). ...... Symptoms include inattentiveness and having difficulty getting (30) , as well as easily becoming distracted. Sometimes, A.D.D. is accompanied by (31) In these cases, the sufferer exhibits excessive physical activity. Psychostimulant drugs can be given to A.D.D. sufferers to assist them with the (32) of desired thought processes, although they might cause (33) Current theory states that medication is the only (34) that has a sound scientific basis. This action should only be taken after an accurate diagnosis is made. Children with A.D.D. do not necessarily have trouble learning; their problem is that they involuntarily (35) their attention elsewhere. It is not only (36) that are affected by this condition. Failure to treat A.D.D. can lead to lifelong emotional and behavioral problems. Early diagnosis and treatment, however, are the key to (37) overcoming learning difficulties associated with A.D.D.

side effects	successfully	completion	adults
medicine	switch	drug	Ritalin
hyperactivity	organized	losing weight	A.D.H.D.
children	attention	remedial action	paying

Questions 38 - 40
You are advised to spend about 5 minutes on Questions 38 - 40.
Refer to Reading Passage 13, and decide which of the following pieces of advice is best suited for child listed in the table below.

Write your answers in boxes 38 - 40 on your Answer Sheet.

ADVICE:
A   current treatment ineffective - suggest increased dosage of Ritalin.
B   supplement diet with large amounts of vitamins and minerals.

C   probably not suffering from A.D.D. - suggest behavioral counseling.
D   bone manipulation to realign bones in the skull.
E   EEG Biofeedback to self-regulate the child's behavior.
F   daily dose of Ritalin in place of expensive unproven treatment.

	CHILD 1	CHILD 2	CHILD 3
Problems	does not listen to given instructions loses interest easily cannot complete tasks quiet and withdrawn	often forgets to do homework sleeps in class disturbs other students	excessively active unable to pay attention dislikes mental effort disturbs other students
Current Treatment	EEG Feedback	none	diet contains no food additives low dose of Ritalin
Best Advice	(38)...............	(39).................	(40)................

READING PASSAGE 14

Questions 1-12
You are advised to spend about 20 minutes on Questions 1-12 which are based on the following reading passage:

THE BEAM-OPERATED TRAFFIC SYSTEM

The Need for Change
The number of people killed each year on the road is more than for all other

types of avoidable deaths except for those whose lives are cut short by

tobacco use.   Yet road deaths are tolerated - so great is
our need to travel about swiftly and economically. Oddly, modern vehicle
engine design - the combustion engine - has remained largely unchanged
since it was conceived over 100 years ago. A huge amount of money and
effort is being channeled into alternative engine designs, the most popular
being based around substitute fuels such as heavy water, or the electric
battery charged by the indirect burning of conventional fuels, or by solar
power. Nevertheless, such innovations will do little to halt the carnage on
the road. What is needed is a radical rethinking of the road system itself.

Section (ii)
The Beam-Operated Traffic System, proposed by a group of Swedish
engineers, does away with tarred roads and independently controlled
vehicles, and replaces them with innumerable small carriages suspended
from electrified rails along a vast interconnected web of steel beams
crisscrossing the skyline. The entire system would be computer-controlled
and operate without human intervention.

Section (iii)
The most preferable means of propulsion is via electrified rails atop the
beams. Although electric transport systems still require fossil fuels to be
burnt or dams to be built, they add much less to air pollution than the
burning of petrol within conventional engines. In addition, they help keep
polluted air out of cities and restrict it to the point of origin where it can be
more easily dealt with. Furthermore, electric motors are typically 90%
efficient, compared to internal combustion engines, which are at most 30%
efficient. They are also better at accelerating and climbing hills. This
efficiency is no less true of beam systems than of single vehicles.

Section (iv)
A relatively high traffic throughput can be maintained - automated systems can react faster than can human drivers - and the increased speed of movement is expected to compensate for loss of privacy. It is estimated that at peak travel times passenger capacity could be more than double that of current subway systems. It might be possible to arrange for two simultaneous methods of vehicle hire: one in which large carriages (literally buses) run to a timetable, and another providing for hire of small independently occupied cars at a slightly higher cost. Travelers could order a car by swiping a card through a machine, which recognizes a personal number code.

Section (v)
Monorail systems are not new, but they have so far been built as adjuncts to existing city road systems. They usually provide a limited service, which is often costly and fails to address the major concern of traffic choking the city. The Beam-Operated Traffic System, on the other hand, provides a complete solution to city transportation. Included in its scope is provision for the movement of pedestrians at any point and to any point within the system. A city relieved of roads carrying fast-moving cars and trucks can be given over to pedestrians and cyclists who can walk or pedal as far as they wish before hailing a quickly approaching beam-operated car. Cyclists could use fold-up bicycles for this purpose.

Section (vi)
Since traffic will be designated an area high above the ground, human activities can take place below the transit system in complete safety, leading to a dramatic drop in the number of deaths and injuries sustained while in transit and while walking about the city. Existing roads can be dug up and grassed over, or planted with low growing bushes and trees. The look of the city is expected to improve considerably for both pedestrians and for people using the System.

Section (vii)
It is true that the initial outlay for a section of the beam-operated system will be more than for a similar stretch of tarred road. However, costs for the proposed system must necessarily include vehicle costs, which are not factored into road-building budgets. Savings made will include all tunnels, since it costs about US $120,000 per kilometer to build a new six-lane road tunnel. Subway train tunnels cost about half that amount, because they are smaller in size. Tunnels carrying beamed traffic will have a narrower cross-sectional diameter and can be dug at less depth than existing tunnels, further reducing costs.

Objections
The only major drawbacks to the proposal are entrenched beliefs that resist change, the potential for vandalism, and the loss of revenue for car manufacturers. Video camera surveillance is a possible answer to vandalism, while the last objection could be overcome by giving car manufacturers beam-operated vehicle building contracts. 60% of all people on earth live in cities; we must loosen the immediate environment from the grip of the road-bound car.

Questions 1-4
You are advised to spend about 5 minutes on Questions 1 - 4.
Refer to Reading Passage 14 "The Beam-Operated Traffic System", and complete the flowchart below with appropriate words or phrases from the passage. Write your answers in boxes *1 - 4* on your Answer Sheet.

Current City Traffic System :

internal combustion engine	independently controlled vehicles	conventional tarred road system	traffic choking the city

Proposed City Traffic System :

.........(1)......	......(2)........	.....(3)......	city
rails	-controlled carriages	System	without any .....(4)....

Questions 5 - 9

You are advised to spend about 8 minutes on Questions 5-9. Choose the most suitable heading from the list of headings below for the seven sections of Reading Passage 14 "The Beam-Operated Traffic System". Write your answers in boxes 5 - 9 on your Answer Sheet.

List of Headings
A.   Returning the city to the people
B.   Speed to offset loss of car ownership
C.   Automation to replace existing roads
D. A safe and cheap alternative
E.   The monorail system
F.   Inter-city freeways
G. Doing the sums (*Example*)
H. The complete answer to the traffic problem
I.   Cleaner and more efficient

5. Section (ii).............. Q8. Section (v)................

6. Section (hi).............. Q9. Section (vi) ....

7. Section (iv).............. Example: Section (vii).........

Questions 10-12

You are advised to spend about 7 minutes on Questions 10 -12.

Refer to Reading Passage 14, and look at the statements below.

Write S if the statement is Supported by what is written in the passage, and write NS if the statement is Not Supported. Write your answers in boxes 10 -12 on your Answer Sheet.

Example: The combustion engine was designed over 100 years ago.   S

10.   The increased speed of traffic in a Beam-Operated Traffic System is due to electric motors being 90% efficient.

11.   Beamed traffic will travel through tunnels costing less to build than subway tunnels.

12.   A possible solution to willful damage to the System is to install camera equipment.

READING PASSAGE 15

You are advised to spend about 20 minutes on Questions 16-26.

BENEATH THE CANOPY

1. The world's tropical rainforests comprise some 6% of the Earth's land area and contain more than half of all known life forms, or a conservative estimate of about 30 million species of plants and animals. Some experts estimate there could be two or even three times as many species hidden within these complex and fast- disappearing ecosystems, scientists will probably never know for certain, so vast is the amount of study required.

2. Time is running out for biological research. Commercial development is responsible for the loss of about 17 million hectares of virgin rainforest each year - a figure approximating 1% of what remains of the world's rainforests.

3. The current devastation of once impenetrable rainforest is of particular concern because, although new tree growth may in time repopulate felled areas, the biologically diverse storehouse of flora and fauna is gone forever. Losing this bountiful inheritance, which took millions of years to reach its present highly evolved state,
would be an unparalleled act of human stupidity.

4. Chemical compounds that might be extracted from yet-to-be-discovered species hidden beneath the tree canopy could assist in the treatment of disease or help to control fertility. Conservationists point out that important medical discoveries have already been made from material found in tropical rainforests. The drug aspirin, now synthesised, was originally found in the bark of a rainforest tree. Two of the most potent anti- cancer drugs derive from the rosy periwinkle discovered in the 1950s in the tropical rainforests of Madagascar.

5. The rewards of discovery are potentially enormous, yet the outlook is bleak. Timber-rich countries mired in debt, view potential financial gain decades into the future as less attractive than short-term profit from logging. Cataloguing species and analysing newly-found substances takes time and money, both of which are in short supply.

6. The developed world takes every opportunity to lecture countries which are the guardians of rainforest . Rich nations exhort them to preserve and care for what is left, ignoring the fact that their wealth was in large part due to the exploitation of their own natural world.

7. It is often forgotten that forests once covered most of Europe. Large tracts of forest were destroyed over the centuries for the same reason that the remaining rainforests are now being felled - timber. As well as providing material for housing, it enabled wealthy nations to build large navies and shipping fleets with which to continue their plunder of the world's resources.

8. Besides, it is not clear that developing countries would necessarily benefit financially from extended bioprospecting of their rainforests.

Pharmaceutical companies make huge profits from the sale of drugs with little return to the country in which an original discovery was made.

9. Also, cataloguing tropical biodiversity involves much more than a search for medically useful and therefore commercially viable drugs. Painstaking biological fieldwork helps to build immense databases of genetic, chemical and behavioural information that will be of benefit only to those countries developed enough to use them.

10. Reckless logging itself is not the only danger to rainforests. Fires lit to clear land for further logging and for housing and agricultural development played havoc in the late 1990s in the forests of Borneo. Massive clouds of smoke from burning forest fires swept across the southernmost countries of South-East Asia choking cities and reminding even the most resolute advocates of rainforest clearing of the swiftness of nature's retribution.

11. Nor are the dangers entirely to the rainforests themselves. Until very recently, so-called "lost" tribes - indigenous peoples who have had no contact with the outside world - still existed deep within certain rainforests. It is now unlikely that there are any more truly lost tribes. Contact with the modern world inevitably brings with it exploitation, loss of traditional culture, and, in an alarming number of instances, complete obliteration.

12. Forest-dwellers who have managed to live in harmony with their environment have much to teach us of life beneath the tree canopy. If we do not listen, the impact will be on the entire human race. Loss of biodiversity, coupled with climate change and ecological destruction will have profound and lasting consequences.

Questions 16-20

You are advised to spend about 8 minutes on Questions 16-20.

Refer to Reading Passage 15 "Beneath the Canopy" and answer the following questions. The left-hand column contains quotations taken directly from the reading passage. The right-hand column contains explanations of those quotations. Match each quotation with the correct explanation. Select from the choices A - F below and write your answers in boxes 16 - 20 on your Answer Sheet.

Example: ' a conservative estimate'

......B......

Quotation	Explanation
Ex: 'a conservative estimate' (paragraph 1)	A. with many trees but few financial resources
16. 'biologically diverse storehouse of flora and fauna' (paragraph 3)	B. purposely low and cautious reckoning
17. 'timber-rich countries mired in debt' (paragraph 5)	C. large-scale use of plant and wildlife
18. 'exploitation of their own natural world' (paragraph 6)	D. profit from an analysis of the plant and animal life
19. 'benefit financially from extended bioprospecting of their rainforests' (paragraph 8)	E. wealth of plants and animals
20. 'loss of biodiversity' (paragraph 12)	F. being less rich in natural wealth

Questions 21-23

You are advised to spend about 5 minutes on Questions 21-23. Refer to Reading Passage 2, and look at Questions 21-23 below. Write your answers in boxes 21 - 23 on your Answer Sheet.

Q21. How many medical drug discoveries does the article mention?

Q22. What two shortages are given as the reason for the writer's pessimistic outlook?

Q23. Who will most likely benefit from the bioprospecting of developing countries' rainforests?

Questions 24-26

You are advised to spend about 7 minutes on Questions 24-26. Refer to

Reading Passage 15, and decide which of the answers best completes the sentences.

Write your answers in boxes 24-26 on your Answer Sheet.

Q 24. The amount of rainforest destroyed annually is:
a) approximately 6% of the Earth's land area
b) such that it will only take 100 years to lose all the forests
c) increasing at an alarming rate
d) responsible for commercial development

Q 25. In Borneo in the late 1990s:
a) burning forest fires caused air pollution problems as far away as Europe
b) reckless logging resulted from burning forest fires
c) fires were lit to play the game of havoc
d) none of the above

Q 26. Many so-called "lost" tribes of certain rainforests:
a) have been destroyed by contact with the modern world
b) do not know how to exploit the rainforest without causing harm to the environment
c) are still lost inside the rainforest
d) must listen or they will impact on the entire human race.

READING PASSAGE 16

You are advised to spend about 20 minutes on Questions 1-15.

DESTINATIONS FOR INTERNATIONAL ENGLISH STUDENTS

Paragraph (i)
At any given time, more than a million international students around the world are engaged in the study of the English language in a predominantly English-speaking country. The five most popular destinations, in order of popularity, are the U. S., Britain, Australia, New Zealand, and Canada. The reasons for choosing to study English abroad differ with each individual, as do the reasons for the choice of destination.

Paragraph (ii)

Numerous studies conducted in Britain and the United States show that the country of choice depends to a large extent on economic factors. While this should not provoke much surprise, careful analysis of the data suggests that students and their parents are most influenced by the preconceptions they have of the countries considered for study abroad, which, in turn, influence the amount they or their parents are prepared to outlay for the experience. The strength of international business connections between countries also gives a good indication of where students will seek tuition. In the main, students tend to follow the traditional pattern of study for their national group.

Paragraph (iii)

The United States attracts the most diverse array of nationalities to its English language classrooms - this heterogeneity being largely due to its immense pulling power as the world's foremost economy and the resulting extensive focus on U.S. culture. Furthermore, throughout the non-European world, in Asia and North and South America especially, the course books used to teach English in most elementary and high schools introduce students to American English and the American accent from a very early age. Canada also benefits from worldwide North American exposure, but has the most homogenous group of students - most with French as their first language. Before furthering their English skills, students in Europe study from predominantly British English material; most Europeans, naturally, opt for neighbouring Britain, but many Asian, Middle-Eastern, and African students decide upon the same route too.

Paragraph (iv)

Australia and New Zealand are often overlooked, but hundreds of thousands of international students have discovered the delights of studying in the Southern Hemisphere. The majority are Asian for reasons that are not difficult to comprehend: the proximity of the two countries to Asia, (Jakarta, the capital of Australia's closest Asian neighbor, Indonesia, is only 5506 kilometers from Sydney), the comparatively inexpensive cost of living and tuition, and, perhaps of most importance to many Asian students whose English study is a prelude to tertiary study, the growing awareness that courses at antipodean universities and colleges are of an exceptionally high standard. In addition, revised entry procedures for overseas students have made it possible for an increasing number to attend classes to improve their English for alternative reasons.

Paragraph (v)

Australia and New Zealand have roughly the same mix of students in their language classrooms, but not all students of English who choose these countries are from Asia. The emerging global consciousness of the late twentieth century has meant that students from as far as Sweden and Brazil are choosing to combine a taste for exotic travel with the study of English 'down under' and in 'the land of the long white cloud'. But even the Asian economic downturn in the 1990s has not significantly altered the demographic composition of the majority of English language classrooms within the region.

Paragraph (vi)

Nor have the economic problems in Asia caused appreciable drops in full-time college and university attendances by Asian students in these two countries. This is partly because there has always been a greater demand for enrolment at Australian and New Zealand tertiary institutions than places available to overseas students. In addition, the economic squeeze seems to have had a compensatory effect. It has clearly caused a reduction in the number of students from affected countries who are financially able to study overseas. However, there has been a slight but noticeable shift towards Australia and New Zealand by less wealthy Asian students who might otherwise have chosen the United States for English study.

Paragraph (vii)

The U.S. and Britain will always be the first choice of most students wishing to study the English language abroad, and it is too early to tell whether this trend will continue. However, economic considerations undoubtedly wield great influence upon Asian and non-Asian students alike. If student expectations can be met in less traditional study destinations, and as the world continues to shrink, future international students of English will be advantaged because the choice of viable study destinations will be wider.

Questions 1-4

You are advised to spend about 5 minutes on Questions 1-4.

Complete the missing information in the table below by referring to Reading Passage 1
"Destinations for International English Students".
Write your answers in boxes 1 - 4 on your Answer Sheet. The first one has been done for you as an example.

	U.S.	Britain	Australia	New Zealand	Canada
order of popularity	1st	*Ex:*... 2nd ...	3rd	4th	5th
type of English in course books used in this country	American	1......	2........	not given	not given
student heterogeneity (1 = most heterogenous 5 = least heterogenous)	1	2	3.......	Equal 3	5

You are advised to spend about 5 minutes on Questions 4 -9.

Choose the most suitable heading from the list of headings below for the seven paragraphs of Reading Passage 1 "Destinations for International English Students". Write your answers in boxes 5 - 10 on your Answer Sheet.

List of Heading

A. Heterogeneity in the language classroom

B. Enrollment demand in Australia & New Zealand.

C. Reasons for the choice of destination

D. The attractions of studying in the antipodes

Example: E. Conclusion

F. Additional student sources

G. Student destinations

Q 4. Paragraph (i) ....   Q 5. Paragraph (ii) ....
Q 6. Paragraph (iii)...............   Q 7. Paragraph (iv)...............
Q 8. Paragraph (v)...............   Q 9. Paragraph (vi)...............

Example: Paragraph (vii) ...... E..............
Questions 10-15
You are advised to spend about 10 minutes on questions 10 -15.
Refer to Reading Passage 1 "Destinations for International English Students", and look at the statements below.

Write your answers in boxes 10 -15 on your Answer Sheet.
Write T if the statement is True; F if the statement is False; N if the information is Not Given in the text.

Example: There are presently more than 1,000,000 foreign students of English abroad.

T   F   N

Q10. Study destination choices are mostly influenced by proximity to home.

T   F   N

Q11. Students who wish to study business will probably study English overseas.

T   F   N

Q12. Students of the same nationality usually make similar study choices.

T   F   N

Q13. English language classrooms in the U.S. have the widest range of student nationalities.

T   F   N

Q14. Standards at Australian and New Zealand tertiary institutions are improving.

T   F   N

Q15. Despite the 1990s Asian economic crisis, Asian students still dominate the English language classrooms of Australia and New Zealand.

T   F   N

READING PASSAGE 17

You are advised to spend about 20 minutes on Questions 32 - 40.
The Danger of ECSTASY

Use of the illegal drug named Ecstasy (MDMA) has increased alarmingly in Britain over the last few years, and in 1992 the British Medical Journal claimed that at least seven deaths and many severe adverse reactions have followed its use as a dance drug. 14 deaths have so far been attributed to the drug in Britain, although it is possible that other drugs contributed to some of those deaths. While it is true that all drugs by their very nature change the way in which the body reacts to its environment and are therefore potentially dangerous, it is still unclear whether the casual use of Ecstasy is as dangerous as authorities believe. What is certain is that the drug causes distinct changes to the body which, unless understood, may lead to fatal complications in certain circumstances.

In almost all cases of MDMA-related deaths in Britain, overheating of the body and inadequate replacement of fluids have been noted as the primary causes of death. Yet in the United States, studies appear to implicate other causes since no deaths from overheating have yet been reported. It seems that normal healthy people are unlikely to die as a result of taking MDMA, but people with pre-existing conditions such as a weak heart or asthma may react in extreme ways and are well-advised not to take it.

Not all physical problems associated with the drug are immediate. Medium-term and long term effects have been reported which are quite disturbing, yet not all are conclusively linked to the drug's use. Medium-term effects include the possibility of contracting the liver disease hepatitis or risking damage to the kidneys. However, animal studies show no such damage (although it is readily admitted by researchers that animal studies are far from conclusive since humans react in different ways than rats and monkeys to the drug), and cases of human liver or kidney damage have so far only been reported in Britain. Nonetheless, evidence to date suggests that alcohol and Ecstasy taken at the same time may result in lasting harm to bodily organs.

Evidence that MDMA causes long-term cellular damage to the brain has, until recently, been based on experiments with animals alone; the most common method of detection is to cut out a section of the brain, and measure the level of the chemical serotonin. This is performed weeks or months after use of a suspect drug. If the serotonin level, which is lowered as a result of the use of many drugs, fails to return to normal, then it is probable that the drug in question has caused damage to the cells of that part of the brain. Ecstasy has been implicated in causing brain damage in this way, but in most cases, the serotonin level returns to normal, albeit after a long time.

Early experiments with monkeys, in which they were found to have permanent brain damage as a result of being administered MDMA, were used to link brain damage in humans to Ecstasy use. These early concerns led to the drug being classified as extremely dangerous, and although the results of the research were doubted by some and criticised as invalid, no attempt was made to change the classification. However, the latest available data regarding permanent brain damage in humans who have taken Ecstasy regularly over many years (as little as once a week for four years) seem to justify the cautious approach taken in the past. The psychological effects of taking Ecstasy are also a major cause for concern. It is clear that the mind is more readily damaged by the drug than is the body. It is not difficult to find occasional or regular users of the drug who will admit to suffering mental damage as a result. Paranoia, depression, loss of motivation and desire, bouts of mania - all are common, and not unusual side effects of the drug.

To be fair to those who claim that Ecstasy frees the personality by removing one's defences against psychological attack, it is true that the drug can be liberating for some users. Unfortunately, the experience is likely to be short-lived, and there is always the danger is that one's normal life might seem dull by comparison.*

Perhaps the most damning evidence urging against the use of Ecstasy is that it is undoubtedly an addictive substance, but one that quickly loses its ability to transport the mind, while it increases its effect upon the body. Yet, unlike the classic addictive drugs, heroin, opium, morphine and so on, Ecstasy does not produce physical withdrawal symptoms. In fact, because one becomes quickly tolerant of its effect on the mind, it is necessary to forgo its use for a while in order to experience again its full effect. Any substance which produces such a strong effect on the user should be treated with appropriate respect and caution.

You are advised to spend about 10 minutes on Questions 32 - 35.
Refer to Reading Passage 17 "The Dangers of Ecstasy", and decide which of the answers best completes the following sentences.
Write your answers in boxes 32 - 35 on your Answer Sheet.
The first one has been done for you as an example.

Example: In recent years, the use of the illegal drug Ecstasy in Britain:
   a) has increased
   b) has decreased alarmingly
   c) has decreased
   d) has increased a little

32. It is not known whether:
   a) drugs change the way the body reacts
   b) the British Medical Journal has reported seven deaths caused Ecstasy
   c) Ecstasy alone was responsible for the 14 deaths in Britain
   d) Ecstasy causes changes to the body

33. The use of Ecstasy:
   a) is usually fatal
   b) is less dangerous than the authorities believe
   c) is harmless when used as a dance drug
   d) none of the above

34. Deaths from Ecstasy are sometimes caused by:
   a) people with pre-existing conditions
   b) too much fluid in the body
   c) overheating of the body
   d) all of the above

35. MDMA studies conducted on animals:
   a) show damage to the kidneys
   b) cannot provide absolute proof of the effect of the drug on humans

c) are cruel and have been discontinued

d) have yet to indicate a long-term brain damage

Questions 36 - 40

Using information from Reading Passage 17, complete the following sentences using NO MORE THAN THREE WORDS.

Write your answers in boxes 36 - 40 on your Answer Sheet.

36. Permanent damage to the body may result if Ecstasy is taken simultaneously with

37. Cellular damage to the brain is detected by measuring the amount of

38. The serotonin level of Ecstasy users takes a long time to

39. One of the positive effects of taking Ecstasy is that it can

40. Ecstasy produces no withdrawal symptoms even though it is

ANSWER SHEET

Reading Passage 01:

1.YES
2. NO
3. NO
4. NOT GIVEN
5. vi
6. iii
7. i
8. ii
9. will(/may) not survive, [or, will (/ may/ could) become extinct]
10. locality/ distribution
11. logging takes place/ logging occurs
12. B

Reading Passage 02:

27. C
28. C
29. A
30. E
31. C
32. A
33. Pairs
34. shapes

35. sighted
36. sighted
37. deep
38. blind
39. similar
40. B

Reading Passage 03:

16. Y   17. Y   18. NG   19. N   20. N   21. NG   22. Y   23. B   24. C   25. A   26. A   27. D   28. E   (26, 27, 28 In any order)

Reading Passage 04:

27. No
28. Not Given
29. Yes
30. No
31. Yes
32. Not Given
33. C
34. A
35. B. (Extra work is offered to existing employees.)
36. D. (Benefits and hours spent on the job are not linked)
37. F. (Longer hours indicate greater commitment to the firm.)
38. G. (Managers estimate staff productivity in terms of hours worked.)
[Answer 35 - 38, in any order]

Reading Passage 05:

1. xi

2. vii

3. v

4. i

5. ix

6.ii

7.x

8.NO

9.YES

10.NG

11.NO

12.YES

13.NG

Reading Passage 06:

1. NOT GIVEN 2. NO 3. YES 4. YES 5. NO 6. South African 7. French 8. Spanish 9. temperate 10. early spring 11. two to five / 2-5 12. sub-tropical 13. South African tunneling/tunnelling

Reading Passage 07:

1. FALSE 2. FALSE 3. TRUE 4. TRUE 5. FALSE 6. NOT GIVEN 7. TRUE 8. NOT GIVEN 9. M 10. E 11. G 12. P 13. J 14. B

Reading Passage 08:

14. viii
15. ii
16. iv
17. ix
18. vii
19. 1946
20. (the) wealthy (members) (of) (society)
21. social, economic, environmental
22. (the) 1970s
23. NOT GIVEN
24. YES
25. NO

26. NO
27. NOT GIVEN

Reading Passage 09:

30.   sustamable 31.   biodegradable   32.   virgin fibre/ pulp   33.
governments/ the government   34.   advances 35.   quality 36.
contaminants 37.   offices 38.   sorted 39.   (re)pulped 40.   de-
ink/ remove ink/ make white   41.   refined

Reading Passage 10:

1. NO   2. NO   3. NO   4. YES   5. NOTGIVEN   6. NO   7. YES   8. (local)
busunesses   9.(work/working) schedule/ rostering/ roster(s)   10.
excessive   11. voluntary absence / absenteeism   12. twenty / 20   13.
Communication

Reading Passage 11:

1. iv   2. i   3. v   4. vii   5. B   6. D   7. A   8. A 9. B   10. E   11.
B   12. E   13. F   14. G

Reading Passage 12:

29. iv
30. vii
31. iii
32. v
33. vi
34. B
35. F
36. YES
37. No
38. NOT GIVEN

39. YES
40. D

Reading Passage 13:

27. a   28. d   29. c   30. organised   31. hyperactivity   32. completion   33. side effects   34. remedial action   35. switch   36. children   37. successfully   38. F   39. C   40. A

Reading Passage 14:

1. electrified   2. computer   3. Beam-Operated Traffic   4. roads   5. C   6. I   7. B   8. H   9. A   10. NS   11. S   12. S

Reading Passage 15:

16. E   17. A   18. C   19. D   20. F   21. 3   22. time (and) money   23. pharmaceutical companies / developed countries   24. b   25. d   26. A

Reading Passage 16:

1. British   2. not given   3. (equal) 3   4. G   5. C   6. A   7. D   8. F   9. B   10. F   11. N   12. T   13. T   14. N   15. T

Reading Passage 17:

32. c   33. d   34. c   35. b   36. alcohol   37. (the chemical) serotonin   38. return to normal   39. free the personality / liberate someusers / remove one's defenses   40. addictive